THE
ART OF
DISTILLING

REVISED & UPDATED

THE
ART OF
DISTILLING

REVISED & UPDATED

AN ENTHUSIAST'S GUIDE TO THE
ARTISAN DISTILLING OF WHISKEY,
VODKA, GIN, AND OTHER
POTENT POTABLES

Edited by Bill Owens, Alan Dikty, and Andrew Faulkner of the

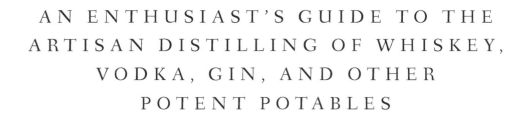

The Quarto Group

Inspiring | Educating | Creating | Entertaining

Brimming with creative inspiration, how-to projects, and useful information to enrich your everyday life, quarto.com is a favorite destination for those pursuing their interests and passions.

Quarry Books titles are also available at discount for retail, wholesale, promotional, and bulk purchase. For details, contact the Special Sales Manager by email at specialsales@quarto.com or by mail at The Quarto Group, Attn: Special Sales Manager, 100 Cummings Center, Suite 265-D, Beverly, MA 01915, USA.

ISBN: 978-1-63159-554-7

Digital edition published in 2019

Originally found under the following Library of Congress Cataloging-in-Publication Data
Owens, Bill.
The art of distilling whiskey and other spirits : an enthusiast's guide to the artisan distillers of potent potables / edited by Bill Owens, Alan S. Dikty and Andrew Faulkner.
p. cm.
Includes index.
ISBN-13: 978-1-59253-569-9
ISBN-10: 1-59253-569-0
1. Distillation. 2. Liquors. 3. Artisans. I. Dikty, Alan S. II. Title.
TP156.D5O94 2009
663'.5—dc22
2009016457
ISBN-13: 978-1-59253-569-9
ISBN-10: 1-59253-569-0

Design and layout: Burge Agency
Cover Image: Shutterstock
Photo Editor: Andrew Faulkner
Illustration: Catherine Ryan

DEDICATION

In fond memory of our friend
Michael Jackson, who is, we
have no doubt, now enjoying his
well-deserved angel's share of
the world's barrels of maturing
whiskey.

CONTENTS

FOREWORD
by Fritz Maytag

8

INTRODUCTION
TO THE SECOND
EDITION
by Bill Owens

10

Chapter 1
A BRIEF
HISTORY OF
DISTILLING

12

Chapter 2
THE
DISTILLING
PROCESS

26

Chapter 3
WHISKEY

48

Chapter 4
VODKA

80

Chapter 5
GIN

92

Chapter 6
BRANDY AND
EAU DE VIE

104

Chapter 7
RUM

120

Chapter 8
TEQUILA
AND AGAVE
SPIRITS

132

Chapter 9
INFUSED
SPIRITS:
Liqueurs, Schnapps,
Anise, and Bitters

140

Chapter 10
DISTILLING
RESOURCES

148

ABOUT THE
CONTRIBUTORS

169

ACKNOWLEDG-
MENTS AND
ABOUT THE
AUTHORS

170

INDEX

171

FOREWORD

by Fritz Maytag

THE SECOND Whiskey Rebellion is happening in the United States, and it is already spreading around the world. In this marvelous book, Bill Owens, Alan Dikty, Andrew Faulkner and their contributors—like intrepid war correspondents—take you to the front lines. You will find here an up-to-the-minute report on the excitement, creativity, and brash enthusiasm of the United States' craft distillers.

I have known Bill Owens since his early involvement in the U.S.'s microbrewing renaissance: He was one of the movement's most fervent innovators. His own achievements are many, and his enthusiasm for the whole wild explosion of brewing creativity is evidenced in his obvious enjoyment of the successes of his brewing colleagues.

The craft-brewing renaissance, of course, began in the 1960s. By the early '90s, it was inevitable that it would evolve into a craft-distilling renaissance. And so, Bill and his cohorts are at it again, now celebrating a small-distillery revolution and the variety and creativity that is springing up everywhere. Yes, we now have "craft" whiskey distillers, experimenting with all facets of grain distilling. And, as with the brewing revolution, the consumer reaps the rewards. We are entering a golden age for the spirits lover, and *The Art of Distilling Whiskey and Other Spirits: An Enthusiast's Guide to the Artisan Distilling of Potent Potables* is an indispensable guidebook to its beginnings.

Detail of the fermenting process of making bourbon, Woodford Reserve Distillery.

Charring oak barrels at Bluegrass Cooperage.

Where did the craft-distilling phenomenon originate? You could say that it came down from the mountains, where pot-distilled whiskeys made by hand—in secret folds— have never entirely disappeared. Or you could say that it came up from the vineyards and orchards, where for many years there has been a tiny craft-distilling segment of superb, hand-crafted fruit brandies and eaux-de-vie. Just know that a second Whiskey Rebellion is upon us and that it is happening right now in a little building near you. And if you have picked up this book already knowing about the great food awakening and hoping for a guide to distilling, you have found it!

What particularly fascinates me about the distillation of alcohol is the enduring mystery surrounding its origins. Distillation itself is a physical art with a long—and colorful—history. And the distilling of all sorts of materials for myriad purposes is an ancient process. But when did the production of distilled spirits as a beverage begin? You are welcome to your opinion, and good luck finding anyone to agree with you! No matter what you think, I encourage

you to savor the eternal enigma that is embodied in a distilled spirit. It is a form of magic to take fruit or grain, ferment it, put it in a pot, heat it and make it disappear entirely, and then watch it reappear, drop by drop, as a clear, volatile, almost ethereal liquid. And it is a dangerous liquid—do not kid yourself. It can catch fire, it can explode, and abusing it can ruin lives. It is powerful, mysterious stuff, surely one reason that it captures the imagination of the producers and consumers swirling and swilling around the current awakening.

So drink deep of Bill, Alan, and Andrew's guide, get on the road with them, go exploring and learning, and enjoy being an early participant in the movement. And take my word for it, as a distiller of whiskey since the second Whiskey Rebellion's first shot: "Heads we win, tails we win!"

Fritz Maytag, Anchor Distilling, San Francisco, April 2009

INTRODUCTION
TO THE SECOND EDITION

by Bill Owens

AS A YOUNG MAN in the 1970s, I had long hair, a Volkswagen Beetle, a hip wife, and a career as a newspaper photographer. I also published four photography monographs, including the classic *Suburbia* (still in print), and I received a Guggenheim Fellowship in photography and three National Endowment for the Arts grants. My dream was to work for *Life* magazine or *National Geographic*, and I ended up stringing for the Associated Press and covered the Hell's Angels beating people with pool cues at Altamont. While all this was happening, I was homebrewing in the garage.

By the 1980s, when I reached middle age, I had a flattop, sold the VW and cameras, and lost a wonderful wife. In 1982, I opened the first brewpub in the United States: Buffalo Bill's Brewery in Hayward, California. The beer was good. My pumpkin ale is still being brewed by many breweries. My public image was "colorful," and the news media loved me. I started believing my own press clips. I opened two more brewpubs and launched a public stock offering to fund the building of a large-scale production brewery. It all seemed like a good idea at the time. It was, after all, "Morning in America," Reagan was in the White House, and the operative phrase for the times was "Greed is good."

I wanted success, money. I had three brewpubs. I grossed a million dollars that year, but I had to pay sixty employees and ended up with no profit. Things don't always work out as you dream. The stock offering never got off the ground, and one by one, the brewpubs were sold off, with Buffalo Bill's being the last to go. But I'll always have Alimony Ale ("The bitterest beer in America!").

By the 1990s, I had gray hair and a new wife, and I was publishing two magazines: *American Brewer* and *Beer: The Magazine*. Once again, my timing was good and *American Brewer* rode the first great wave of craft brewing. Things were looking great, but financially, the two magazines turned out to be not such a great idea. I soon stopped publishing *Beer* and sold *American Brewer*.

Soon after, the AARP mailings started showing up, and I opened an antique store. That venture lasted 6 months. Then my literary agent sold some *Suburbia* photographs to Elton John, giving me enough money for a (used) Lexus and the cash for a 3-month trip across America, so I ran away from home. On this trip, I decided to visit some craft distilleries. I was intrigued, and the creative juices started to flow again. When I returned to California, I founded the American Distilling Institute (ADI). In 2003, I held the first ADI distilling conference at St. George/Hangar 1 Distillery, and eighty people showed up.

AUTHOR'S NOTE ON SPELLING
For reasons that have yet to be adequately explained, American and Irish distillers spell the word whiskey with an e, while their Scotch, Canadian, Japanese, and New Zealand peers spell whisky without it.

Research on *The Art of Distilling Whiskey and Other Spirits* started in 2006.

In 2007, I decided to make another trip across America. Again, the trip was funded by selling photographs to museums, an assortment of art galleries and friends in the United States and in Europe. This second trip (21,000 miles) took 4 months, and from fifty-three DVDs of images, we selected 100 or so for the first edition of this book. Does anybody remember DVDs?

Ten years ago, the original edition of *The Art of Distilling Whiskey and Other Spirits* was published, and 500 people attended the American Distilling Institute (ADI) conference at St. George distillery in Alameda, CA. The 2018 conference had 2,000 attendees from seven different countries.

That's just the beginning of the changes that have occurred in the last 10 years. As the growth of craft distilling has been around 30% a year, craft distilling is not about to slow down or peak anytime soon. The U.S. government's Alcohol and Tobacco Tax and Trade Bureau licenses approximately two new distilled spirits plants for each working day. Craft distilleries are popping up in the UK, Europe, Australia, South Africa, and many other countries. There is even a craft distillery on St. Helena in the South Atlantic, one of the most remote islands in the world.

Vodka is no longer the darling of craft distilling. Now, it is whiskey and gin. As of early 2018, there are over 1,500 licensed craft distilleries in the USA, and at least 700 ferment, distill and bottle their own spirits. A significant number of them grow their own corn, rye, and barley. Whiskey is the flavor of the week, month, and year for now and for the foreseeable future. The latest generation of craft distillers is using a beer-style wash to produce whiskey. I can assure you the marriage of brewery-distillery is going to happen.

Next to whiskey, gin has seen tremendous growth. You can say it has caught on in a big way. There are now dozens of distillers barrel-aging gin, a process that sets you apart from standard gins and gives you flavor and romance. The new generation of gins is wonderful, and there are more than 500 gin producers.

Spirits pundits predict brandy will come back. The problem with brandy is that only a few states have wineries able to produce grapes suitable for brandy. However, apple brandy, brought to you by Johnny Appleseed, is following on the tails of apple cider as the next resurging category. With Washington, New York, Michigan, and Pennsylvania leading the charge, American applejack has a patriotic ring to it that few distillers can resist.

With 400 craft distillers making rum, it is not far behind gin and whiskey. Many distillers are using sugarcane juice and molasses produced by American sugarcane farmers. The resulting spirits are wonderful. I still have a foot in both camps, photography and distillation. But if I had to choose, it'd be distilling, because it's a way of life, and the craft-distilling industry is really about lifestyle. People take great pride in producing spirits. This book is a look at craft distillers and the rest of the whiskey, rum, vodka and gin industry.

Special thanks to Alan Dikty, the coauthor and editor of this book, and a personal friend. Alan has been with me as a friend and writer for some 40 years. Alan knows spirits.

And finally, a big thank-you to Andrew Faulkner. He also started with me through photography and, after a decade and a half with ADI, is now editor and publisher of *Distiller* magazine.

Bill Owens. Hayward. California. March 2009

Chapter 1
A BRIEF HISTORY OF DISTILLING

Very Fine Whiskey bottle, circa the 1920s: This vintage bottle was acquired *empty* at a flea market.

SINCE the earliest known use of distillation about 5,000 years ago, practice of the art has grown and spread around the world in several waves, the speed and extent of each being dictated by geography, trade routes and cultural and religious influences. Each successive wave gave rise to significant technical advances in distillation, making it less expensive, more efficient, and more controllable.

Possibly the earliest written record of distillation is in the *Epic of Gilgamesh*, which describes a form of essential oil distillation practiced in Babylon as far back as 3000 BC. Herbs were placed in a large heated cauldron of boiling water, and the cauldron's opening was covered with a sheepskin, fleece side down. Periodically the sheepskin was changed, and the condensate soaking the fleece was wrung out into a small jar. Essential oils floated to the surface of the water collected in the jar and were skimmed off. Medieval texts and woodcuts show the same principle being used to concentrate alcoholic vapors from boiling wine. (Incidentally, this is similar in principle to a method that the Phoenicians used for consuming cannabis.)

These woodcuts from *The Art of Distillation* by Jonathan French (1651) show a small part of the wide variety of forms distilling equipment had taken by the seventeenth century. Two key improvements are shown: multiple distillations in one setup (one still feeding into the next), below, and an improved vapor condenser (a coil of tubing known as a "worm" in a barrel of cold water), left.

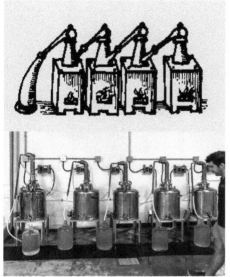

DISTILLING MIGRATES EAST AND WEST

By 500 BC, alcohol distillation was an established industry in the ancient Indian area known as Taxila (in modern northwest Pakistan), where archaeologists discovered a perfectly preserved terra-cotta distillation system. In this process, steam rising from a pot of boiling water passed through a bed of fermented grains, picking up alcohol and flavors from the grains. The vapors then struck the bottom of a second pot filled with cold water, where they condensed and dripped into a collection tube.

From Taxila, knowledge spread to the East and the West, and by 350 BC, knowledge of the distilling process appeared in the writing of Aristotle in Greece and Sinedrius in Libya. The first arrival of distillation technology in China is misty, but by AD 25, bronze stills of similar design were being produced and used there.

By the end of the first millennium AD, the practice of distillation had spread throughout northern Africa and the Middle East. The process had advanced significantly over this 1000-year period, and the material being distilled was now boiled directly in a large sealed pot, which had a long tube leading from its apex to a small collection jar. When the Moors invaded Spain, they brought this technology with them, and soon the genie (or spirit) was out of the bottle. The technology spread from Spain to Italy in AD 1100, and was recorded in Ireland by 1200, Germany by 1250, and France by 1300. England, Scotland, Poland, Russia, and Sweden joined the club by 1400.

DISTILLING TECHNOLOGY EVOLVES

European exploration and conquest spread rapidly around the world, carrying the technology of distillation with it. The first stills in the Americas appeared not long after the conquistadores, and the Portuguese brought the technology to Japan by 1500.

This technology was largely controlled by monasteries and alchemists, who continuously experimented and improved on the equipment. By the mid-1600s, several texts had been published on the subject of distillation, a sample of which included the woodcuts on this spread, from *The Art of Distillation* by Jonathan French (1651). As this information spread beyond clerical and scientific circles, wealthy individuals began to establish stillhouses on their estates.

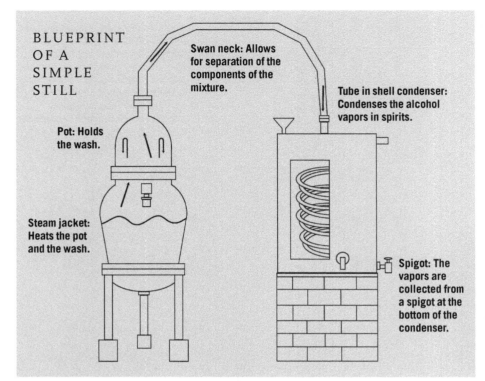

BLUEPRINT OF A SIMPLE STILL

Swan neck: Allows for separation of the components of the mixture.

Pot: Holds the wash.

Steam jacket: Heats the pot and the wash.

Tube in shell condenser: Condenses the alcohol vapors in spirits.

Spigot: The vapors are collected from a spigot at the bottom of the condenser.

As knowledge blossomed throughout the Renaissance, distillation continued to develop rapidly. Distillation was removed from the exclusive province of scientists, monks, and professionals and became a common household art. Recipe books abounded.

By the 1700s, the complexity and sophistication of commercial-scale distilling equipment had advanced rapidly. Advances in the understanding of how distillation actually worked led to new still designs that could make better quality spirits more easily and faster than in the past. Distilling became more accessible to the masses, and the monopoly held by the church and the elite classes was threatened. These centers of power soon enacted restrictions, at first to protect that monopoly, and later purely for revenue.

REGULATION AND REBELLION

Since 1700, the regulation and control of distillation has been mostly a story of lost freedoms and rights. A few rays of sunshine have since poked through the clouds. The elite and governments of Europe tried repeatedly to exploit and control distillation. In England, for example, the first taxation of commercial distillation appeared in 1690 to pay for a war with France. Private distillation was exempted from this tax, and it remained free from interference as taxes and regulations were raised, lowered, abolished, and resurrected over the next century. Private distillation in England flourished and grew significantly during this time (and perhaps not a little of this product found its way into commercial channels via the back door), until it was outlawed in 1781 to enhance the collection of revenue. The massive Gin Craze of early eighteenth-century Great Britain had its roots, in part, in this unfettered spread of distillation.

The Whiskey Rebellion in western Pennsylvania.

The United States government's first attempt to tax distillation resulted in the Whiskey Rebellion of 1791, which was put down by federal troops led by George Washington (who was serving as president at the time).

Federal excise taxes were abolished after the end of the War of 1812, only to be imposed during the Civil War in the 1860s (and continue to this day).

Napoleon introduced regulation in France. The laws varied widely over the next century, but stabilized in 1914, when the right was granted to anyone with a vineyard or orchard to distill up to 20 liters of spirits from their fruit if they agreed to pay a tax. This right was originally inheritable, but that was revoked in the 1950s. This system led to the development of traveling stills, known as *bouilleurs de cru*, which were once very common sights in the French countryside. Because the number of permitted individuals has shrunk with every passing year, very few of these mobile distilleries remain.

Australians lost their right to home-distill their own beverages in the aftermath of World War I, again as a revenue measure.

Many African, Latin American, and southern European nations have continued to allow private distillation under a wide variety of rules, ranging from none, through inspection of stills, to onerous regulations and high taxation. In general, traditional alcoholic beverages are made in most farmhouses using traditional equipment (mostly pot stills of various forms), without any adverse effects on society.

One countertrend to this march of increased government regulation was the legalization of private, noncommercial distilling by New Zealand in 1996. The New Zealand government found that the expense of enforcing the ban on private distillation far outweighed the revenue coming from fines, so the law was abolished. This change led to widespread adoption of small-scale distilling as a hobby, and, as hobbyists always will, they experimented with equipment and techniques continuously. This boom in home distilling in New Zealand did not go unnoticed, and starting around the turn of the 21st century, a new generation of licensed commercial craft distilleries started to open in North America, the United Kingdom, and parts of Europe.

FUTURE TRENDS

Just as the appearance of microbreweries followed the renaissance of homebrewing, increasing the choices and level of quality for all beer drinkers, craft distilleries are starting to thrive around the world, using new equipment and methods. Many of these modern small distilleries are experimenting with new types and categories of spirits, creating novel and sometimes uniquely local spirits.

The first modern craft distilleries, such as St. George Spirits, Germain-Robin, Jepson Vineyards, and Clear Creek Distillery were established in the 1980s, closely following the growth curves of family wineries after Prohibition and the growth of craft breweries following Fritz Maytag's purchase of Anchor Brewing. Since around 2000, exponential growth has followed the pattern of a classic industry resurgence and is expected to continue for years to come.

The U.S. movement has garnered so much excitement that it has inspired similar proliferation of distilleries and brands in Canada, Ireland, Scotland, England, France, Australia, India, South Africa, and many other countries around the globe.

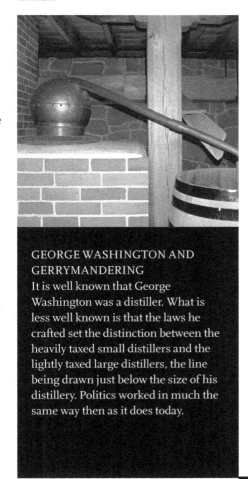

GEORGE WASHINGTON AND GERRYMANDERING
It is well known that George Washington was a distiller. What is less well known is that the laws he crafted set the distinction between the heavily taxed small distillers and the lightly taxed large distillers, the line being drawn just below the size of his distillery. Politics worked in much the same way then as it does today.

A tombstone that was used during Prohibition for stashing moonshine near Morgantown, West Virginia

MOONSHINE

The cultural stereotype of "corn likker" moonshine being made by hillbillies deep in the woods in Southern states was never quite the final word on moonshine production in the United States. Anywhere fruit or grain is grown, illicit spirits were distilled for home use and informal commercial sale. The heyday of large-scale moonshine production was during U.S. Prohibition of the 1920s and 1930s, when all of the United States and parts of Canada were officially dry. But illegal moonshine production still continues on a reduced scale to this day. Some of it is produced by increasingly sophisticated home distillers, and yes, there are still backwoods moonshiners, even if some of those seem to exist primarily to appear on cable network television shows.

Alas, times (and moonshine) are not what they used to be. Modern moonshiners tend to skip the grain mashing and go directly to fermentation by dissolving regular sugar in warm water, fermenting the sugar water with baker's yeast and then distilling off the resulting alcohol. The results are spirits much inferior to a distilled grain spirit, and ultimately an arrested moonshiner. The Alcohol and Tobacco Tax and Trade Bureau (TTB, also known as "the Feds") keeps track of the sale of large quantities of bulk sugar, particularly in rural areas with a past history of moonshining, although a surprising amount of this "sugarshine" is made, or at least produced for sale in what are sometimes delicately referred to as urban ethnic markets, particularly in the mid-Atlantic states.

You have been warned.

A POS card advertising Junior Johnson's Midnight Moon by Piedmont Distillers

Specially Crafted Catdaddy Carolina Moonshine by Piedmont Distillers, Madison, NC.

DIRT TRACK DISTILLING

—

Students of American popular culture know that moonshine whiskey and NASCAR go together like actor Burt Reynolds and muscle cars. Starting in 1973 with the movie *White Lightning*, Reynolds made a career of portraying Southern good ol' boys delivering moonshine in fast cars, while outrunning the local sheriff.

The real-life inspiration for such cinema characters was Robert Glen Johnson Jr. (born in 1931 in Wilkes County, North Carolina), better known as Junior Johnson. Johnson was a moonshiner in the rural South who became one of the early superstars of NASCAR in the 1950s and '60s.

Johnson grew up on a farm and developed his driving skills running moonshine as a young man. He consistently outran and outwitted local police and federal agents in auto chases, and he was never caught while delivering moonshine to customers.

Johnson became something of a legend in the rural South, where his driving expertise and "outlaw" image were much admired. Johnson is credited with inventing the "bootleg turn," in which a driver escapes a pursuer by sharply putting his speeding car into a 180-degree turn on the highway, then speeding off in the opposite direction before his pursuer can turn around. Johnson was also known to use police lights and sirens to fool police roadblocks into thinking that he was a fellow policeman; upon hearing his approach, the police would quickly remove the roadblocks, allowing Johnson to escape with his moonshine.

In 1955, Johnson decided to give up delivering moonshine for the more lucrative (and legal) career of being a NASCAR driver. Unfortunately, the "Revenuers" had not forgotten Junior. In 1956, federal agents found Johnson working at his father's moonshine still and arrested him. Johnson was convicted of moonshining and was sent to federal prison, where he served

11 months of a 2-year sentence. He returned to the NASCAR scene in 1958 and picked up where he left off. He went on to win fifty NASCAR races in his career before retiring in 1966.

In 1965, writer Tom Wolfe wrote an article about Johnson in Esquire magazine. The article, originally titled "Great Balls of Fire," turned Johnson into a national celebrity and led to fame beyond his circle of NASCAR fans. In turn, the article was made into a 1973 movie based on Johnson's career as a driver and moonshiner titled *The Last American Hero*. Jeff Bridges starred as the somewhat fictionalized version of Johnson, and Johnson himself served as technical advisor for the film.

More recently, Johnson's family has licensed the Junior Johnson name for use in promoting a legal distilled product: Junior Johnson's Midnight Moon from Piedmont Distillers in Madison, North Carolina.

DON'T TRY THIS AT HOME
(NUDGE, NUDGE, WINK, WINK, SAY NO MORE)

Soon after national Prohibition began in the 1920s, a person could walk into virtually any grocery store in the United States and find for sale brick-size blocks of compressed raisins bound together with condensed grape juice. Attached to the block was a small container of dried yeast. The wrapping contained the following text:

"WARNING: Do not dissolve this fruit brick in warm water and then add the contents of the yeast packet, as this will result in fermentation and the creation of alcohol, the production of which is illegal."

Needless to say, the local A&P sold a lot of fruit bricks while Prohibition was in force.

Traditional moonshine starts out with the production and fermentation of what is basically a simple beer. Traditionalists would create a mash of ground corn, hot water, and enough malted barley to provide sufficient enzymes to convert the starch in the grains into simple sugars. Once the starch conversion was complete, yeast was added to the mash, with the resulting fermentation turning the sugars into alcohol. The fermented mash would then be boiled in the pot still to distill off the alcohol.

Virginia Lightning Corn Whiskey by
Belmont Farm.

*“WHISKEY IS WHAT
BEER WANTS TO BE
WHEN IT GROWS UP.”*

Virginia Lightning
Moonshine by Belmont
Farm, Culpeper, VA.

MODERN "MOONSHINERS"

The current interest among hobbyist distillers in creating first-rate liquors, and the general wholesome quality of their products, tracks primarily to several convergent trends:

CRAFT BREWERS

Craft brewers are not simply the first ones to study how to make outstanding small-batch spirits; they are also going to shape the face of micro- and personal distilling. Brewers have already mastered three key skills: how to collaborate, how to organize, and how to drive legislation.

The current interest in distilling among brewers is so widespread that it is virtually impossible to talk to craft brewers who aren't already distilling on the sly, working on permits, or know someone who is. One erstwhile brewer framed his transition from beer to liquor with this aphorism: Whiskey is what beer wants to be when it grows up.

Making beer at home has been legal on a federal level since 1978. For a decade or so after it was permitted, homebrewers (in the United States) explored all kinds of beer and ale styles they could not purchase through their local stores. They perfected their techniques, competed against each other in

regional and national contests, published their personal recipes, gave out awards to their peers, and later put that knowledge to use by opening brewpubs and craft breweries.

Homebrew supply shops everywhere were selling hops, malts, specialty grains, carboys, esoteric scientific equipment, and lab-cultured yeasts to tens of thousands of homebrewers trying, good naturedly, to best each other in rounds of My Beer Is Better Than Yours.

Chuck Miller stands in front of his pot still at Belmont Farm Distillery (see page 19), one of a dozen distilleries in the United Stated producing a legal moonshine product.

Two generations of Beams at the Limestone Branch Distillery, Lebanon, KY. Right to left, Steve Beam, his father, Jimmy, and his brother, Paul.

By the 1990s, some brewers were pushing the limits of their equipment and ingredients, becoming essentially novice distillers. Their homemade rigs looked pretty much the same as brewing equipment. The ingredients were the same. They were learning on pot stills because, for hundreds of years, variations on that model had been the choice of folk distilling. Most of what a casual researcher found in popular culture references were the big, copper, pumpkin-shaped boilers of a style that would have been familiar to eighteenth-century farmers.

As brewers, they already knew about grains, malt, yeast, enzymes, ideal fermentation temperatures, filtration systems, and the water profiles that lead to great-tasting beverages. Some had come to believe that the only thing stopping them from having whiskey was too much water. Because they had developed widespread networks for sharing information already—books, magazines, contests, clubs, festivals, newsletters, and rudimentary online newsgroups—questions began to circulate about how best to remove that excess water. Sharing, critiquing, and judging were an entrenched part of the culture that was starting to take up what had long been a secret practice. Anonymous online forums were ideal tools for vetting home-distilling questions. Unlike the old Appalachian moonshiners, modern hobby distillers with homebrewing backgrounds were already used to talking to each other online and in person.

NEW ZEALAND

Because few of the twentieth-century books on moonshining held much practical information on techniques for building and operating stills, amateur distillers without a family history in such matters learned by trial and error. Then, in 1996, New Zealand lawmakers scrapped legislation forbidding home distillation, resulting in an explosion of interest and innovation, specifically around the design of home-size stills.

These innovative Kiwi home distillers went online and, because their hobby was legal, started talking to each other openly. Brewers who were getting into distilling, with their already established networks and culture of openness, noticed. They seized on a wealth of new verifiable information coming out of the Southern Hemisphere and added their own experiences, especially in online forums.

Since then, as reliable information has been vetted online about how best to build and operate small-scale stills, home column or reflux, stills have evolved, becoming more compact and efficient, and able to put out as close to pure alcohol as is possible outside a laboratory (in short, very clean stuff). Most recently, a specific style of distilling has evolved that's all about purity, efficiency, and making lots of neutral spirits in very compact column stills.

Apple Pie Moonshine
by Baldwin Distilling Co.,
Mitchell ACT 2911,
Australia.

MOONSHINE DEFINED

The original definition of moonshine is any liquor made from unregistered stills by unlicensed distillers. This definition covers a Kentucky farmer making the liquor his father did, a New York imbiber wresting 10 ounces (296 ml) of gin from a case of Budweiser, as well as a San Francisco chef tweaking her grandmother's kümmel to carry on the tradition.

More recently, the growth of the licensed craft-distilling industry has resulted in the anomaly of legal, branded moonshine, labeled as such, or as "white whiskey" or "white dog." Such unaged white spirits can be packaged and sold quickly, which helps the cash flow of new start-up distilleries.

Home distilling does continue, however, and now falls into three loose categories—economic, technical, and artisanal producers.

Virginia Sweetwater Moonshine by Virginia Sweetwater Distillery, Marion, VA.

Milk Can Moonshine by
Backwards Distilling Co.,
Mills, WY.

Mayday Moonshine by Durango Craft Spirits, Durango, CO.

A variety of products by MB Roland Distillery, Pembroke, KY.

ECONOMIC DISTILLERS

Economic distillers make liquor because homemade is cheaper than store bought. Any type of still might be used, from an inherited copper pot still, to modern reflux models or even an aquarium heater in a plastic bucket. They are apt to distill sugar spirits, but also grains and fruits when they may be had inexpensively. Although their products are prone to be of questionable quality, they are not necessarily bad liquor—think of marc and grappa made from pomace that might otherwise be thrown away.

TECHNICAL DISTILLERS

Technical distillers are armchair (or even professional) engineers and chemists, gearheads who strive to make the most efficient distillery setup they can, forever tweaking and adjusting their rigs, creating technological wonders. They run and rerun a batch of spirits to create the purest spirit they can, taking meticulous notes of every temperature fluctuation, proof variation, and yield. Technical distillers tend to have an inordinate amount of vodka on hand because the end result of their frequent experiments is often a high-proof, nearly pure spirit they can supplement with extracts and essences for the exact flavor they want.

ASPIRING AND ACCOMPLISHED ARTISANS

Aspiring and accomplished artisans comprise the third group, whose goal is to make authentic and great-tasting spirits. While technical distillers consider unwanted chemical compounds obstacles to pure liquor, artisans rightfully regard taste and aroma as the backbone that defines their own personal style of distilling. They tend to use less-efficient, old-school pot stills—they might immediately recognize the kind that a farmer used in 1740. Some use column stills, but without the columns at maximum efficiency, thus preserving taste and aroma by not distilling to the highest proof possible.

DIAGRAM OF A COLUMN DISTILLER

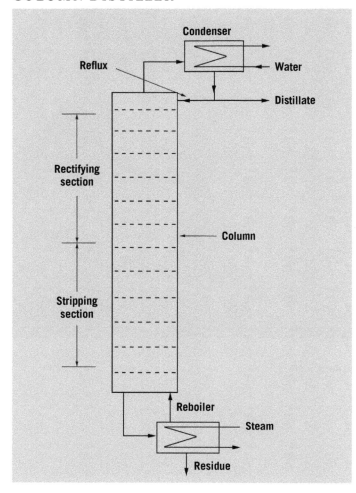

This flowchart illustrates how the wash is transformed into spirits. The bottom of the still strips out the water, while the rectifying section (top of the still) distills the liquor to increase its alcohol percentage.

DIMENSIONS OF A TYPICAL SPIRITS STILL

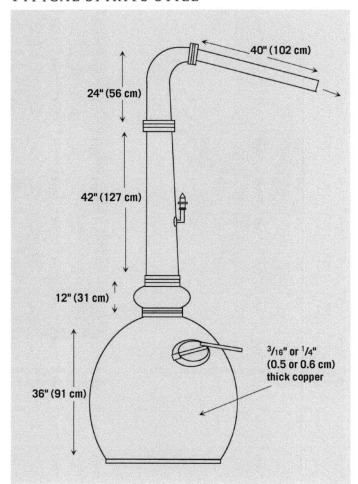

A pot is wider than tall, allowing vapors to escape from the wash. A tall swan neck allows for separation of the components of the mixture. The shape of the still affects the flavor components of the spirits. Every pot still is unique, as distillers want distinctive flavor profiles in their finished spirits.

ANATOMY OF A POT STILL

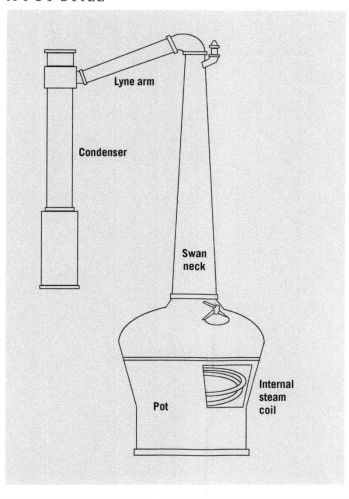

As illustrated here, a whiskey still has four parts: pot, swan neck, lyne arm and condenser. The shape of each affects rectification and the flavor of the spirit.

POT: The pot can by any shape: round, onion or conical. The shape of the pot affects how the wash is heated (always to 172°F [78°C]). It can be heated by direct fire, steam, gas, or wood. Most pots have a sight glass so the distiller can check for foaming during the distillation process.

SWAN NECK: The swan neck sits on top of the pot. It can be tall, short, straight, or tapered. Often, the swan neck is connected to the pot via an ogee, a bubble-shaped chamber. The ogee allows the distillate to expand, condense and fall back into the pot during distillation. Most pot stills have a tapered swan neck, allowing for better separation and better enriching of the spirits during distilling.

LYNE ARM: The lyne arm sits on top of the swan neck. It can be tilted up or down, and it can be tapered or straight. Often pot stills are fitted with a dephlegmator or purifier. Its main purpose is the enrichment of spirits before they're sent on to the condenser.

INTERNAL STEAM COIL: The internal steam coil heats the wash to 173°F (78°C), where the alcohol separates from the wash.

CONDENSER: The condenser, or worm, is used for cooling the spirits and providing a small stream to a collection tank or pail.

ECONOMICAL INGREDIENTS FOR DISTILLING

Consider a glut of plums for backyard slivovitz or a skid of dried fruit at bargain pricing that can be turned into Arabian siddiqui. However, ersatz whiskeys made from breakfast cereals are not unheard of, so caveat emptor is the rule.

A fruit *eau de vie* fermentation at Stringer's Orchard Wild Plum Winery & Distillery

Chapter 2

THE DISTILLING PROCESS

IN THE MOST literal sense of the word, distillation means the concentration of the essence of a substance by separating it from any other substances that it is mixed with. In the case of distilling alcohol, this means boiling a fermented liquid in a still and condensing the vapor back into a liquid to separate the ethanol from the solids, water, and other chemical compounds in the fermented solution. But just as the devil is in the details, the art of distilling is in how the distiller achieves that separation and how precise that separation is.

The wide range of stills described in this chapter each originally evolved to meet the requirements of producing a particular type of spirit. Depending on the type of spirit being made, precision is not necessarily the goal of the distiller. Thousands of chemical compounds are created by fermentation and distillation, all of which can have, for better or worse, an effect on the ultimate taste or character of a distilled spirit. The distiller's primary job is to retain the desired flavor elements, while discarding those that are not. This is not as simple as it sounds. And despite all of the high-tech controls in a modern distillery, the still master nevertheless has the final call.

Spirits dancing on one of the plates of a rectification column.

HOW DISTILLATION WORKS

Distillation is a physical process in which compounds are separated by virtue of their different boiling points. Two compounds with the same boiling point occurring together would not be separable by distillation. Fortunately, such occurrences with the ingredients in liquor and spirits are rare.

The separation in distillation occurs when a mixture of compounds in the still is brought to a boil. Compounds with lower boiling points vaporize at lower temperatures than compounds with higher boiling points. This means that the vapor, or steam, rising off the boiling mixture is richer in the lower-boiling-point compounds than in the higher-boiling-point ones. Next, this vapor

is collected and cooled to condense it back into a liquid. The resulting liquid, called the distillate, contains a considerably higher concentration of the lower-boiling-point compounds than of the higher-boiling-point ones.

In a simplified example, let's consider a mixture of 90 percent water and 10 percent ethanol. Water has a boiling point of 212°F (100°C), and ethanol has a boiling point of 173.1°F (78.4°C). The ethanol will boil and vaporize well before the water, so when the vapors are collected and condensed, the resulting distillate will have a high concentration of ethanol and comparatively little water. The distillate will not be pure ethanol because some water will vaporize at the boiling point of ethanol, even if the

water itself is not at its boiling point. Tails start at 203°F (95°C) and contain a high percentage of fusel alcohols, known to distillers as wet dog bouquet. A little bit is actually needed in some types of whiskey, but only a little bit. Think Islay Scotch Whisky.

Because all the compounds in a still will vaporize to a greater or lesser extent during boiling, the separation of the compounds will not be perfect, so more elaborate stills have been developed to intensify the separation of the vapors once they have left the kettle. In modern high-separation stills, this is done by employing a reflux column to manage the vapors after they leave the kettle and before they are condensed and drawn from the still.

A STILL'S BLUEPRINT

The whiskey still has four parts: pot, swan neck, lyne arm and condenser. The shape of each section affects rectification (redistillation) and the taste of the spirits. There is no perfect design; each manufacturer says its pot still makes the best-tasting whiskey.

At this point, distilling is an "art." To make good whiskey, you need to have good ingredients (clean wash) and a good palate (nose and tongue), and you need to know when to start and stop (making heads and tails cuts). When it comes to whiskey distilling, the process is controlled by a distiller not a computer or a manual. The pot can be any shape: round, onion, or conical. The shape of the pot affects how the wash is heated (to 172°F [77.8°C]). It can be heated by direct fire, steam, gas, or wood. All systems have advantages and disadvantages. There is no right way to heat wash. Most manufacturers, however, prefer a double-jacketed steam-water system that provides a gentle heat to the wash. Mainly, you don't want to burn the wash. Most pots have a sight glass so the distiller can check for foaming during the distillation process.

The swan neck sits on top of the pot. It can be tall, short, straight or tapered. Often the swan neck is connected to the pot via an ogee, sometimes called a "lampglass," which is a bubble-shaped chamber. The ogee allows the distillate to expand, condense, and fall back into the pot during distillation. Most pot stills have a tapered swan neck, allowing for better separation and better enriching of the spirits during distilling.

The lyne arm sits on top of the swan neck. It can be tilted up or down, and it can be tapered or straight. Most arms are tapered down. Often pot stills are fitted with a dephlegmator or what Scottish distillers call a purifier. The dephlegmator is fitted with baffles that use water plates or tubes to cool the distillate, sending most of it back into the pot. Its main purpose is the enrichment of the spirits before they're sent on to the condenser.

The condenser, or worm, is used for condensing the vapor back to a liquid and entraining a small stream to a collection receiver.

THE CHEMISTRY OF PURE SPIRITS

Even a modern high-separation still cannot produce pure ethanol. This is because water forms an azeotrope with ethanol. An azeotrope is a mixture of two liquid compounds whose molecules become loosely bonded such that they have a common boiling point that is different from either constituent's. In the case of ethanol and water, the azeotrope occurs at a mixture of 96.5 percent ethanol and 3.5 percent water, and it has a boiling point of 172.67°F (78.15°C). This is 0.45°F (0.17°C) lower than the 173.12°F (78.4°C) boiling point of pure ethanol. In distillation, this azeotrope is a single compound with a boiling point of 172.67°F (78.15°C), and the still proceeds to separate it on that basis. The ethanol that is purified by a fractionating column is not, therefore, pure 100 percent ethanol but pure 96.5 percent ethanol, with the "impurity" being pure water. No amount of redistillation under the conditions discussed here will influence this percentage; 96.5 percent alcohol by volume (ABV) is the theoretical maximum purity that can be derived by this process.

The temperatures stated above are at standard atmospheric pressure. In a column still, due to increased pressure at the bottom resulting from the pressure drop over the plates, the temperatures would be quite a bit higher than stated. For example, the spent wash, which would have a boiling point of about 212°F (100°C) at standard pressure, would have a boiling point of about 220°F (104.4°C) due to the increased pressure.

A small pot still, similar to many moonshine stills, is in operation for tourists to see at the Glenmorangie Distillery, Scotland.

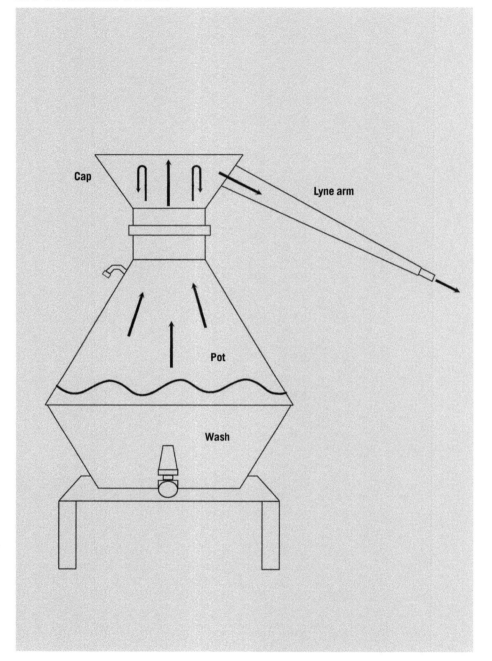

Cap

Lyne arm

Pot

Wash

WHISKEY STILLS IN DETAIL

There are several different designs of stills used for making whiskey. These include the moonshine still, gooseneck still, continuous-run column still, French *Charentais alembic* still, and hybrid pot still. (The traditional English spelling of this French word is alembic.)

In the basic moonshine still, vapors from the heated wash rise into the cap. After hitting the flat top of the still, vapors exit via the lyne arm into the condenser, where they condense and become spirits.

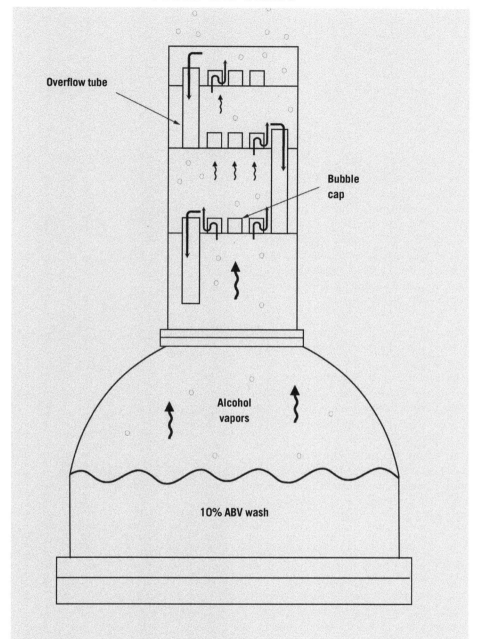

Overflow tube

Bubble cap

Alcohol vapors

10% ABV wash

MOONSHINE STILL

The most basic and rudimentary design is a crude pot still, or moonshine still, which is a closed pot, like a pressure cooker, with a pipe leading from the lid into a condenser coil. The condenser coil can either be long enough to air-cool the vapors, or it can be shorter and immersed in a water jacket. Such a still affords minimum separation of the vapors because there is almost no separation once they leave the kettle. Although this design of still is not suitable for producing beverage alcohol by modern standards, it will still concentrate an 8 or 10 percent ABV (alcohol by volume) wash to 60 percent in a fairly fast run.

There are many home distillers and illicit commercial moonshiners using this type of still today. And, because this type of still is typically heated on a stove top or on a gas burner, it is necessary to remove all suspended solids from the wash before placing it in the pot. To do otherwise would risk burning solids on the bottom of the pot.

The bubble caps sit on a tray over vapor tubes in the column. The caps provide contact between the rising vapors and descending reflux, creating a distilling cycle and enriching the alcohol. Arrows indicate vapors rising from the wash and hitting the bubble caps. A percentage of pure vapors continues to rise and the "less pure" fall back into the still for redistillation.

GOOSENECK STILL

The gooseneck pot still is the most common design of still used to produce Scottish malt whisky. Some Irish whiskeys and a number of American and Canadian whiskeys are also distilled in this type of still. This style of pot still has been in use for centuries for commercial whiskey production, and it is even more popular today in modern whiskey distilleries than ever.

The gooseneck still has a large round kettle and is functionally very similar to the crude pot still, except it has a long, broad neck rising from the kettle that allows enough separation to hold back most of the fusel alcohols from the distillate while retaining the desired flavors in the finished spirit. The neck bends at the top and connects to a pipe called a lyne arm that leads to a condenser coil immersed in water. The lyne arm usually angles downward slightly toward the condenser, but in some distilleries it tilts upward.

The level of separation in a gooseneck pot still is affected by the amount of condensation that takes place in the neck and lyne arm that falls back into the kettle. This condensation is called reflux, and the more reflux, the higher the level of separation. If the lyne arm is angled downward, then any vapor in the lyne arm that condenses will fall forward toward the condenser and become part of the distillate passing to the receiver. However, if the lyne arm is angled upward, condensation falls back to the kettle and will create additional reflux and, therefore, additional separation.

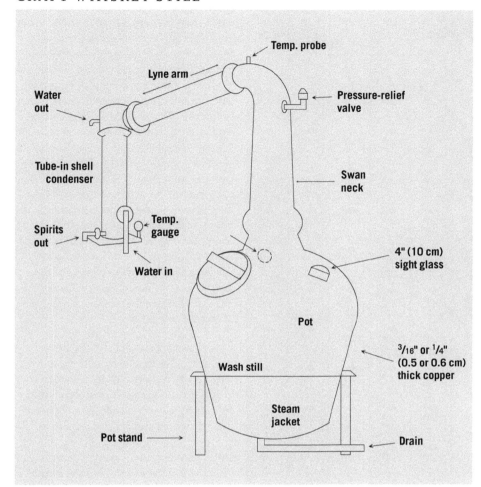

Model of a gooseneck Forsyths whisky still.

Not all craft whiskey stills are
alike, but most share the same
basic construction.

BEVERAGES PRODUCED IN GOOSENECK STILLS

Because the long, broad neck provides a large surface area, which results in a larger proportion of reflux than crude pot stills, gooseneck stills are more suitable for distilling beverage alcohol. The gooseneck stills are suited to the production of whiskey, brandy, rum, schnapps, and other non-neutral spirits, for which they are widely used commercially. However, they are not suitable for the production of vodka, gin, or other spirits derived from neutral alcohol, which requires a high-separation still capable of producing pure azeotrope ethanol.

The wash distilled in gooseneck stills is typically separated from the suspended solids, much like the malt washes used for making Scottish malt whisky. Some gooseneck stills are heated by an open fire under the kettle, which would result in the burning of suspended solids if they were in the wash. However, most contemporary stills are heated with steam jackets. This, combined with a rummager, can enable these stills to boil full mashes with all the grain in the kettle without burning the solids on the bottom of the pot.

A rummager is an agitating device that slowly turns around inside the still pot, dragging a net of copper chains along the bottom of the kettle to prevent solids from caking up and burning during distilling.

As the wash runs down through the trays of the column, it encounters the hot steam, which vaporizes the compounds in the wash and carries them up the column. The lower-boiling compounds continue to rise up the column while the higher-boiling ones condense and are carried down the column. The column has an exit valve at every tray where vapor can be drawn off and led to a condenser. This enables the operators to configure the system so certain trays lead to a condenser that goes to the heads receiver, another set of trays can be sent to the hearts receiver, and other trays can be sent to the tails receiver. What flows to the bottom of the column is residue that is sent to the drain. A possible configuration for bourbon would have the top two trays configured for heads, then the next four configured for hearts, the next five for tails, and the rest of the trays would reflux with no draw off and what reached the bottom would be discarded as residue.

The draw-off rates would be set up to maintain a hearts fraction with, say, a constant 65 percent ABV. Bourbon that's distilled in a continuous-run column still is usually done in two distillations, both with the hearts drawn off at about 65 percent ABV.

Because a continuous-run still runs for many months at a time, the wash must be fairly clear with a minimum of solids; otherwise, the buildup of residue in the system would become untenable and the system would need to be shut down to be cleaned. So, there is no process with a continuous-run still whereby the entire mash is distilled. The mash must always be strained or filtered before being placed in the reservoir supplying the still.

The distillery must have a battery of fermenters that are in constant operation at each stage of the fermentation process to keep up with the continuous demand for wash for the stills.

CONTINUOUS-RUN COLUMN STILL

This type of still is used for producing enormous volumes of spirit in a continuous operation that runs constantly for up to eleven months straight before it is shut down for cleaning and overhauling. They commonly have a fractionating column that stands about 100 feet (30.5 m) high (similar to that of an oil refinery) and a series of bubble-cap trays spaced every couple of feet (0.8 m) up the column. The trays are farther apart near the bottom and get closer together toward the top. It has no pot or kettle, per se, and it is heated by blasting steam upward from the bottom of the column while the wash is continuously fed into a tray at the middle of the column.

THE CONTINUOUS-RUN DESIGN FLAW

There is an inherent design flaw in this type of still. Because the continuous-run still has a constant flow of new wash coming into it at all times, there are always heads and tails present in the column. This is unlike a batch still, which is any of the noncontinuous stills discussed in this text, where the heads are drawn off at the beginning of the run and then they are gone. In a continuous-run operation, all fractions are constantly being introduced to the column by the incoming wash. This poses no problem with the tails, because at the trays where the hearts are drawn off, the tails are lower in the column and are, therefore, not present to be drawn off with the hearts. However, heads are still present at these trays, so no matter how well a continuous-run still is equilibrated there'll always be a small amount of heads in the hearts fraction.

Having said this, the continuous-run column is a high-separation still that makes very precise separation of the compounds in its column. There is always going to be a trace amount of heads in the hearts, and this amount is still within the allowable limits for potable spirits. In most cases, it is less than the residual heads found in the hearts from commercial batch stills.

FRENCH CHARENTAIS ALAMBIC STILL

This type of still is used almost exclusively for making brandy, including Cognac, Armagnac, Calvados, and other famous French brandies. It is designed especially to leave a lot of the aromatics and flavor in the distillate, and is therefore one of the lower-separation beverage-alcohol stills. Because of this quality, spirits are usually distilled twice in a French Charentais alambic still. Whiskey can also be made in this design of still. It is functionally quite similar to the gooseneck still, but it creates a lower level of separation, making a richer and creamier-tasting whiskey, but with a little more fusel alcohol.

The French Charentais alambic still has three major components: the kettle with helmet, the preheater, and the condenser. The helmet is the chamber just above the kettle, and it serves as an expansion chamber, which works well to hold back a lot of the heavier compounds, such as fusel alcohols and furfurols, while allowing the desirable aromatics and flavors to be carried over into the distillate.

The preheater, as the name implies, preheats the next batch of wine to be distilled. It is also used as a reservoir to enable a near-continuous distillation process. Some brandy distillers simply include them as part of the hearts (not the heads). In this way, continuously feeding wine into the kettle is possible. Because there is no workable way to drain the pot during operation, the continuous feeding of wine must stop when the kettle is too full to take any more.

Alembic still installation in France.

Prior to a distillation run, the preheater is filled with wine to be heated for the next distillation. The preheater has the vapor tube from the pot passing through it on its way to the condenser. This transfers heat from the vapor to the wine before the vapor enters the condenser. This heats the wine in the preheater to near boiling during the distillation run and reduces the amount of heat that the condenser has to dissipate, thereby making efficient use of heat and reducing the amount of cooling water used.

The preheater has a pipe with a valve leading from it to the kettle. When a distillation run is finished and the pot has been drained, the operator can open the valve and fill the kettle with another charge of wine from the preheater that's already at near-boiling temperature. This makes efficient use of heat and significantly reduces the amount of time to bring the next batch of wine to a boil. The condenser in a French Charentais alambic still, as in most types of stills, consists of the copper coil immersed in a water jacket with cold water circulating around it.

BEVERAGES PRODUCED IN ALAMBIC STILLS

These stills are invariably used to distill wine, or in the case of whiskey, distiller's beer. They are not generally used to distill full mashes with all the solids left in. However, design-wise, the Charentais could be used to distill mashes with solids because its kettle is the same as that of the standard alembic, which is widely used to make grappa and marc from grape pomace. To do this, a sieve tray must be inserted into the kettle to serve as a false bottom to hold the solids above the bottom of the pot and prevent burning.

A 2-column, 16-plate hybrid still for vodka production at NOLA Distilling, New Orleans, LA.

HYBRID POT STILL

This type of still is the most versatile of all the stills. Each artisan pot still is nearly made to order, based on a distiller's needs and preferences. Its components include a spherical-shaped kettle, a condenser, and a wide variety of optional components, such as a steam jacket or a direct fire, an agitator, a helmet, one or two columns of bubble-cap trays, a dephlegmator, and a catalyzer.

The spherical-shaped kettle evenly heats the substrate, particularly if there is an agitator. And, a hybrid still that's steam heated and has an agitator can be used to distill any wash. Even washes full of fruit pulp or grain mash can be heated in this configuration of kettle without any risk of burning on the bottom of the pot. Also, by constantly agitating the wash throughout the distillation run, the distillery can save about 20 percent on the heat required to perform the distillation.

The ability to distill the entire wash, including all the solids, purportedly gives a superior flavor to the spirit produced. Apparently, the fruit mashes for making schnapps yield a richer, more complex flavor if they can be distilled with all the fruit pulp in the kettle. Many whiskey distillers contend the same to be true for distilling grain mashes, and almost all brands of American whiskey are distilled with the grain solids in the still.

Twin columns of bubble-cap trays.

The helmet component (optional) is technically an expansion chamber, and it is usually a nearly spherical dome that sits directly on top of the kettle. As vapor rises from the pot, it passes through a comparatively narrow passageway into the larger volume of the helmet. This results in a sudden reduction in vapor velocity, which helps hold back higher-boiling-point compounds while allowing desirable aromatics and flavors to continue up the column. Some distillers say this helmet is key to producing a truly excellent spirit.

From the helmet, the vapor rises into the column. In some hybrid-pot still configurations, the column is mounted directly on top of the helmet. When there is no helmet, the column is mounted directly on top of the kettle. In other configurations, such as two columns, the column is positioned beside the pot. The reason for this is the still would stand too high for most facilities if the column were stacked on top of the helmet or even on top of the kettle. Within the column are bubble-cap trays. The vapor rises up the tubes under the bubble caps and bubbles out from under

the cap and through the standing liquid on each tray. The standing liquid overflows at a certain depth to the next tray below. Compound separation takes place by the redistillation that occurs when the heat from the vapor transfers to the standing liquid. This causes higher-boiling-point compounds in the vapor to condense and lower-boiling-point compounds in the liquid to evaporate. The overall effect is to drive the lower-boiling-point compounds up the column in vapor state and the higher-boiling-point compounds down the column in liquid state.

OPTIONAL STILL COMPONENTS

Modern hybrid stills have an interesting feature that allows the operator to bypass any of the trays to vary the separation level for the column. There are levers on the side of the column connected to each tray, and the operator can position the lever to cause the tray to turn sideways and allow the vapors and liquid to pass by. Or the operator can position the lever the other way to put the tray in place so that it is fully engaged in processing reflux.

The dephlegmator resides above the top bubble-cap tray. It is a chamber at the top of the column with numerous vertical tubes for the vapor to travel through on its way to the condenser. There is a water jacket around the vertical tubes that the operator can flood with cooling water to increase the amount of reflux. The rate of water flow in the dephlegmator can be adjusted to give granular control over the amount of reflux.

Having the capability to dial up or down the reflux creates a great deal of control over the compound mix in the finished spirit. For example, if a given spirit had an excellent aroma and flavor profile but a rough finish due to an excess of fusel alcohol, the reflux could be dialed up slightly to hold back the fusel.

The catalyzer is positioned above the dephlegmator and has an array of "sacrificial" copper. Copper is an important material in a still because the noxious sulfides in the vapor instantly react out upon contact with copper. However, as this occurs over time, the copper material of the still becomes compromised, and expensive still components require replacing. The idea of the catalyzer is to have a chamber with copper in the vapor path specifically designed to react out the sulfides from the vapor. Over time, this copper erodes from

the reaction with the sulfides, but it can be cheaply replaced. In effect, the copper in the catalyzer is being sacrificed to save the copper material of the still.

The catalyzer also reacts out ethyl carbamate (also called "urethane") which is carcinogenic. Ethyl carbamate is generally formed as a result of urea in the fermentation substrate. The amount of natural urea in a fermentation is very low, but over the years urea has been added as a yeast nutrient to provide nitrogen for the yeast.

In summary, hybrid stills can be superb stills and are well known for making quality spirits.

Unfortunately, their throughput is comparatively slow, and distilleries are often put in the position of having to opt for larger throughput stills, such as the continuous-run column, to meet the demands of their markets.

COLUMN CONFIGURATION

The number of bubble-cap trays in the column depends on the intended use of the hybrid still, and it is therefore optional. Some artisan pot stills are used to make vodka and have two tall columns with a total of twenty bubble-cap trays. An excellent configuration for making whiskey, however, would be a still with a helmet, a column with four trays, a dephlegmator and a catalyzer.

Hybrid still.

THE BATCH-STILL PROCESS OF DISTILLATION

THE DISTILLATION process is operationally the same for all four batch stills discussed previously: the moonshine still, the gooseneck still, the French Charentais, and the artisan pot still. The continuois-run column still has a different regimen, and it is described in the section that follows.

HEADS, HEARTS, AND TAILS

In distilling parlance, the compounds in the wash that are not ethanol or water are called congeners. Some congeners, such as acetaldehyde, methanol, and certain esters and aldehydes, have lower boiling points than ethanol; certain other esters, the higher alcohols (fusel alcohols) and water, have higher boiling points than ethanol. This means the lower-boiling-point congeners come out in high concentration at the beginning of a batch distillation run, and the higher-boiling-point ones come out in high concentration toward the end of the run, leaving the ethanol and the most desirable compounds as the most abundant components during the middle of the run. When distillation takes place in a batch still, the distillate that comes out is divided into three fractions called heads, hearts, and tails.

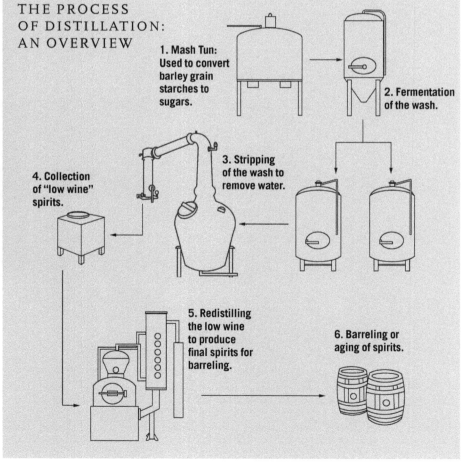

THE PROCESS OF DISTILLATION: AN OVERVIEW

1. Mash Tun: Used to convert barley grain starches to sugars.

2. Fermentation of the wash.

3. Stripping of the wash to remove water.

4. Collection of "low wine" spirits.

5. Redistilling the low wine to produce final spirits for barreling.

6. Barreling or aging of spirits.

THE MAJOR STEPS FROM BARLEY TO BARREL

1. Mash Tun: Used to convert barley grain starches to sugars.

2. Fermentation of the wash.

3. Stripping of the wash to remove water.

4. Collection of "low wine" spirits.

5. Redistilling the low wine to produce final spirits for barreling.

6. Barreling or aging of spirits.

congeners into the finished spirit. However, in flavor-neutral spirits, such as vodka, the goal is to remove as many congeners as possible to end up with a spirit that has a clean, nonspecific palate.

Because both the heads and the tails contain a lot of ethanol and residual desirable flavor, they are mixed together and saved for future recovery. The heads and tails when mixed together are called feints. Feints can be distilled separately to produce another whiskey run, or they can be mixed in with a future spirit run, where their ethanol and flavors are recovered as a part of that run. However, each subsequent distillation produces its own set of heads, hearts, and tails, and the feints from those runs are also saved for future recovery.

TWO-RUN DISTILLATION

When whiskey is made, it is usually done in two distillation runs: a beer-stripping run and a spirit run.

The beer-stripping run is generally done in a larger, high-volume pot still called a beer stripper. The beer stripper is used to distill the fermented wash and concentrate the ethanol and all the impurities into a distillate of about 25 percent ethanol, called low wine.

The spirit run is done in a smaller whiskey still, such as a gooseneck or a hybrid still, called a spirit still. The spirit still is used to distill the low wine and refine it into the finished spirit. There are two outputs retained from the spirit run: the finished spirit and the feints.

The heads contain the unwanted lower-boiling-point congeners that come out at the beginning of the run.

The tails contain the unwanted higher-boiling-point congeners that come out at the end of the run.

The hearts are the desired spirit in the middle.

Because whiskey is not distilled at a high-separation level, it means that each fraction bleeds into the adjacent fraction. That is to say, there is a considerable amount of ethanol in the heads fraction, and there are late-heads congeners at the beginning of the hearts fraction. Similarly, there is a significant amount of early-tails congeners

at the end of the hearts, and there is a considerable amount of ethanol in the tails fraction. The whiskey, comprised mostly of ethanol and water, has a delicate balance of late-heads and early-tails congeners that make up the flavor profile of the whiskey.

There are literally thousands of these congeners, or chemical flavor compounds, created during the distilling process, all of which have the potential of adding to or subtracting from the desired final flavor profile of the distilled spirit. Part of the art (as opposed to the science) of distilling is knowing when these congeners are coming out of the still, and when to add them to the hearts or add them to the feints. In flavor-specific spirits, such as brandy and whiskey, it is desirable to carry over selected

For a beer-stripping run, the fermented wash, which is typically about 8 percent ABV, is loaded into the beer stripper, and the contents are brought to a boil. Because this run is just a primary distillation, the heads, hearts and tails are not separated out. The entire output from this run is collected in a single lot, and the run is continued until the aggregate percent alcohol is down to 25 percent ABV. This distillate is the low wine, which is the input to the spirit run.

To produce the finished whiskey, the spirit still is filled with the low wine from the beer-stripping run and often a measure of feints from previous spirit runs. The spirit still is then brought to a boil.

It is with the spirit run that the distiller adjusts the boil-up rate to achieve a gentle, slow flow of distillate and carefully separates out the heads, hearts, and tails.

SINGLE-RUN DISTILLATION

Some whiskey distilleries produce their whiskey in a single distillation. They do a spirit run directly from the wash. The hybrid stills discussed previously are well suited to this type of whiskey distillation, but it is labor intensive and the distiller must pay a lot of attention to numerous smaller runs rather than one larger run.

Some people find the whiskey from a single-distillation run to be richer and have a more natural flavor, while others find it to be harsh and unrefined. In the following text, the more common double-distillation method is used.

MAKING THE CUTS

Probably the most elusive part of the distilling process for making whiskey is making the cuts from heads to hearts and then to tails. Making a cut from one fraction to the next is the point where the distiller switches the output so that it is collected in a different receiver than the previous fraction. At the end of the spirit run, the heads will be in one container, the hearts in another and the tails in a third one. The question is: when do you switch from one fraction to the next?

Experienced distillers do this by taste. Even though there are measurable parameters, such as still-head temperature and percent alcohol of the incoming spirit that can be used to judge when to make the cuts, taste and smell still remain the most reliable methods for determining them.

Here are the empirical parameters for judging the cuts:

The percent alcohol of the spirit that is flowing out of the still (the incoming spirit)

The still-head temperature

These vary from one still to the next, and they vary based on the properties of the low wine (e.g., percent alcohol and quantity). It is possible to develop a consistent process using the same still and the same quantity and formulation of low wine, such that the parameters remain the same for each run. For example, in a spirit run in a hybrid still with low wine that is 25 percent ABV: Begin-cut (the cut from heads to hearts) is usually done when the evolving distillate is at about 80 percent and when the still-head temperature is about 180°F (82°C). End-cut (the cut from hearts to tails) is often done at about 65 percent and when the still-head temperature is about 201°F (94°C).

However, a spirit distilled from a straight malt wash can often be end-cut as low as 60 percent ABV. Also, a gooseneck still distilling the very same wash may begin-cut at 72 percent ABV and end-cut at 59 percent ABV. Therefore, it is because of these nuances that smell and taste become the only truly reliable indicators of when to make the cuts.

BEGIN-CUT

When making the begin-cut, the taste characteristics that the distiller is looking for are as follows. When a spirit run comes to boil and the first distillate starts flowing from the still, this is the beginning of the heads fraction. The distiller can collect a small sample of the distillate on a spoon or in a wineglass and smell it. At this stage, the distillate will have the sickening smell of solvents (such as nail-polish remover or paint-brush cleaner). However, before long, this solvent smell diminishes, and even when a sample is tasted, these compounds will be very faint. As the solvent character disappears completely, the distillate will start to take on a hint of whiskey. This flavor will increase until it becomes very pronounced and highly concentrated. It is when this flavor is clearly evident, but is still increasing in intensity, that the distiller cuts to the hearts fraction.

END-CUT

To make the end-cut, the distiller needs to monitor the flavor for changes in taste. At the beginning of the hearts fraction, the intensity of the whiskey flavor will still be increasing, and it will continue to do so until it becomes very strong. However, as the hearts continue, the intense whiskey flavor will fade into a smooth, sweet, pleasant flavor that will persist for most of the hearts. The flavor will change slightly as the hearts progress, but it will remain sweet and pleasant. Toward the end of the hearts, the flavor will start losing its sweetness, and a trace of harsh bitterness will begin to appear in the flavor. This harsh, bitter flavor is the onset of the tails. Although a small amount of this bitterness is considered to contribute to the "bite" character of the whiskey, the distiller should cut to the tails receiver before much of it is allowed to enter the hearts.

The tails can be collected until the evolving distillate is down to about 10 percent and the still-head temperature is about 206°F or 208°F (97°C or 98°C). The reason for doing this is to render all the residual alcohol that is left in the still at the end of the hearts fraction. This alcohol can then be recovered in a future spirit run.

The tails fraction starts out bitter and the bitterness becomes more intense as the tails continue, but as the tails progress, the bitterness subsides and gives way to a sweet-tasting water. This sweet water is called backins.

THE CONTINUOUS-RUN PROCESS OF DISTILLATION

In a continuous-run distillation process, wash is constantly entering the column, so all three fractions (heads, hearts, and tails) are present in the column at all times. This means there can't be a discrete cut where the heads are drawn off and the hearts begin, or that the hearts end and the tails begin. All three fractions must be drawn off at the same time.

A continuous-run column is a high-separation fractionating still that separates the compounds very well, so once the still is equilibrated and functioning in its steady state of operation, the distillers can determine which families of compounds are at each tray. For example, they might determine that the compounds coming out of the top two trays are heads compounds and route those two trays to the heads receiver. Similarly, they might observe that the compounds coming out of the next four trays down are hearts. Then they might determine that the five trays below the hearts trays are producing tails and route them to the tails receiver. Below the tails trays just water would be coming out, and the valves would be closed, so it would be left to flow to the bottom of the column and then to a drain.

Because this type of still is not intermittent in its operation, it must be set up to constantly draw the three fractions of distillate at all times. Although this is difficult to set up, it can produce very large quantities of spirit twenty-four hours a day for a long time.

Chapter 3
WHISKEY

> " ALWAYS CARRY A FLAGON OF WHISKEY IN CASE OF SNAKEBITE, AND FURTHERMORE, ALWAYS CARRY A SMALL SNAKE. "
> W.C. Fields, American actor and world-class drinker

THIS chapter introduces the process of distilling a world's worth of whiskeys, including North American styles of bourbon, Tennessee, rye, blended American, corn, and Canadian, and on to Scotch and Irish whiskeys from Europe.

Of all of the basic categories of spirits, whiskey has spread the most across the world, achieving a geographic and stylistic diversity that is unmatched by any other type of distilled spirit. From the basic grain-based distilled spirits of ninth-century Ireland, Scotland and northern Europe have evolved the classic whiskeys of Scotland and Ireland. These spirits, in turn, served as the models for distillers in the newly settled North American colonies to produce what came to be the first modern rye whiskey and then in rapid succession, corn, bourbon, blended American and Canadian whiskies.

All of these now-classic styles of whiskey have, in recent decades, served as the stylistic inspiration for myriad new whiskeys throughout the world, from Germany to Australia and Nepal in between. Some of these new whiskeys are based on existing styles. Japanese whiskey distillers, for example, have generally taken their inspiration (and malt, and sometimes even their water) from Scotland. Others are boldly going forth in new directions, particularly among the new generation of American craft distillers.

THE HISTORY OF BOURBON WHISKEY

Whiskey barrels on the move.

IN the early 1700s, a combination of bad economic times and religious unrest against the Anglican Church in Great Britain set off a wave of emigration from Scotland and Ireland. These Scots, Irish, and so-called "Scotch-Irish" (Protestants from the northern Irish county of Ulster) brought to North America their religion, their distrust of government control, and their skill at distilling whiskey.

This rush, augmented by German immigrants of a similar religious and cultural persuasion, passed through the seaboard colonies and settled initially in Pennsylvania, Maryland, and western Virginia. Mostly small farmers, they quickly adapted to growing rye because of its hardiness and, in the western counties, Native American corn because of its high yields. Grain was awkward to ship to East Coast markets because of the poor roads, so many farmers turned to distilling their crops into whiskey. In Pennsylvania, these were primarily rye whiskeys; farther to the west and south corn whiskeys predominated. By the end of the American War of Independence in 1783, the first commercial distilleries had been established in what was then the western Virginia county of Kentucky. From the start, they produced corn-based whiskeys.

In 1791, the cash-strapped federal government imposed the first federal excise tax on distillers. The farmer-distillers of western Pennsylvania responded violently. Federal tax agents were assaulted and killed by angry mobs. Order was finally restored in 1794 when the federal government sent in an army of 15,000 militiamen, led by George Washington, to put down the revolt. The ringleaders were convicted and sentenced to be hanged. But cooler heads prevailed, and after jail time they were pardoned and released. This situation did provoke a new migration of settlers through the Cumberland Gap and into the then western frontier lands of Kentucky and Tennessee. In these new states, farmers found ideal corn-growing country and smooth limestone-filtered water, two of the basic ingredients of bourbon whiskey.

The name bourbon comes from a county in eastern Kentucky, which in turn was named for the Bourbon kings of France, who had aided the American rebels in the Revolutionary War in the early nineteenth century. Bourbon County was a center of whiskey production and transshipping. (Ironically, at the present time, it is a "dry" county.)

The local whiskey, made primarily from corn, soon gained a reputation for being particularly smooth because the local distillers aged their products in charred oak casks. The adoption of the "sour mash" grain conversion technique further distinguished bourbon from other whiskey styles.

By the 1840s, bourbon was recognized and marketed as a distinctive American style of whiskey, although not as a regionally specific spirit. Bourbon came to be produced in Kentucky, Tennessee, Indiana, Illinois, Ohio, Missouri, Pennsylvania, North Carolina, and Georgia, although the only legal requirement for calling a whiskey "bourbon" is that it be produced in the United States. Nowadays, bourbon production is slowly expanding to other states as new craft-whiskey distillers come online. Initially, bourbon was made in pot stills, but as the century progressed, the new column still technology was increasingly adopted. The last old-line pot still plant closed in Pennsylvania in 1992, but the technique was revived in Kentucky in

1995 when the historic Labrot & Graham Distillery, now known as the Woodford Reserve Distillery, was renovated and reopened with a set of new, Scottish-built copper pot stills. More recently, most of the new generation of craft-whiskey distillers use pot stills.

The late nineteenth century saw the rise of the temperance movement, a social phenomenon driven by a potent combination of religious and women's groups. Temperance societies, such as the Women's Christian Temperance Union and the Anti-Saloon League, operated nationally, but they were particularly active in the southern states. The notion of temperance soon gave way to a stated desire for outright prohibition, and throughout the rest of the century an assortment of states and counties adopted prohibition for varying lengths of time and degrees of severity. This muddle of legal restrictions played havoc in the bourbon industry, because it interfered with the production and aging of stocks of whiskey.

Label for Hudson Baby Bourbon by Tuthilltown Spirits.

Label for Pappy Van Winkle's Family Reserve Kentucky Straight Bourbon Whiskey.

Label for Blanton's Single Barrel Kentucky Straight Bourbon Whiskey by Buffalo Trace Distillery.

WHO'S YOUR WHISKEY DADDY?

The current holy grail of American whiskey brands is the Pappy Van Winkle line of bourbons and rye whiskeys. Yes, there really is, or was, a Julian "Pappy" Van Winkle Sr. (he passed on to his well-deserved reward in 1965 at age 89), but there never was an Old Rip Van Winkle Distillery, and the Stitzel-Weller Distillery in Shively, Kentucky, that Pappy ran closed in 1991. The brand has been produced since 2002 at the Buffalo Trace Distillery under the supervision of Julian Van Winkle III. Other "sourced whiskey" brands have even more tenuous connections to their named distillery. Since the beginning of commercial whiskey production in the British Isles and North America, distilleries have sold finished bulk spirits to each other to make up for production shortfalls or dispose of surpluses. This has been a normal, if not publicly discussed, practice in the distilling industry. A more recent phenomenon has been the rise of brands

with a historical pedegree (Pogue Bros. for example) or marketing concept (Jefferson's Presidential Select), but no actual distillery. The largest distillery in the United States that few whiskey drinkers have ever heard of is a former Seagram's plant in Lawrenceburg, IN, now called MGP of Indiana, which has no brands of its own, but produces and packages over 50 brands of whiskey for other companies, both large (Bulleit Rye and George Dickel Rye) and small (Templeton Rye and many "craft" spirit brands). Matured spirits from distilleries such as MGP allow a number of actual craft distilleries to start up and be able to sell aged whiskeys while they are waiting for their own self-distilled spirits to properly age. Sometimes, the labeling of such brands is a tad vague about where the product inside the bottle comes from, but the alternative is even more too-young craft whiskey on the market than there already is.

Amid the barrels of bourbon, John Pogue reaches for something on the shelves at the Old Pogue Distillery in Maysville, KY.

The Ohio River, as seen from balcony of the Pogue mansion, gave life to Kentucky bourbon by providing a shipping route out to the Mississippi River and down to New Orleans, where it could be shipped internationally. The family house sits above the site of the historical Pogue Distillery and next to the current Old Pogue Distillery.

Labrot & Graham Distillery, now known
as the Woodford Reserve Distillery,
Versailles, KY.

Cask Strength Bloody Red Corn Bourbon by
Wood Hat Spirits, New Florence, MO, earned
Best of Class Whiskey in the American Distilling
Institute's 2018 International Judging of Craft
Spirits.

National Prohibition in 1919 had effects on the bourbon industry beyond shutting down most of the distilleries. Drinking did not stop, of course, and the United States was soon awash in illegal alcohol, much of it of dubious quality. What did change was the American taste in whiskey. Illicit moonshine and imported Canadian whiskies were lighter in taste and body than bourbon and rye. The corresponding increase in popularity of white spirits such as gin and vodka further altered the marketplace. When repeal came in 1933, a number of the old distilleries didn't reopen, and the industry began a slow consolidation that lasted into the early 1990s, at which time there were only ten distilleries in Kentucky and two in Tennessee.

In the last half of the 20th century, almost all bourbon was made in the states of Kentucky, Virginia, and Indiana. But with the resurgence of craft distilleries, bourbon is now being made in most states. Craft producers are increasingly looking toward heirloom strains of corn in their mash bills to create unique flavor profiles, marketing distinctions, and introduce a sense of terroir. Bloody Butcher red corn, Hopi blue corn, and Olathe corn are a few examples. Many distilleries are working with state universities and seed banks to revive cultivation of strains that had fallen out of fashion.

Legendary Master Distiller Jimmy Russel, of Wild
Turkey, shares a belly laugh with Chris Morris,
Master Distiller at Woodford Reserve, during a
bourbon tasting in the Brown Hotel, Louisville,
KY, at the American Distilling Institute's Annual
Conference.

Straight Bourbon Whiskey by Woodinville Whiskey Co., Woodinville, WA.

OYO Sherry-Finished Bourbon Whiskey by Middle West Spirits, Columbus, OH.

Elk Rider Bourbon Whiskey by Heritage Distilling Co., Gig Harbor, WA.

Bourbon Rubenesque by Wood Hat Spirits, New Florence, MO.

Diablo's Shadow Limited Edition California Straight Bourbon Whiskey by Sutherland Distilling Co., Livermore, CA.

Bourbon Whiskey by Sugar House Distillery, Salt Lake City, UT.

TENNESSEE WHISKEY

Barrels at the Corsair Distillery, Nashville, TN.

TENNESSEE whiskey is a first cousin of bourbon, with a virtually identical history. The same sort of people used the same sort of grains and the same sort of production techniques to produce a style of whiskey that, remarkably, is noticeably different. The early whiskey distillers in Tennessee, for reasons that are lost to history, added a final step to their production process when they began filtering their whiskey through thick beds of sugar-maple charcoal. This filtration removes some of the congeners (flavor elements) in the spirit and creates a smooth, mellow palate. The two remaining old-line whiskey distillers in the state continue this tradition, which a distiller at the Jack Daniel's Distillery once described as being "same church, different pew." The newer generation of Tennessee craft-whiskey distilleries are less wedded to tradition and produce a variety of whiskeys, including bourbon and single malt.

Nelson's Green Brier Tennessee White Whiskey by Nelson's Green Brier Distillery, Nashville, TN.

RYE WHISKEY

Dark Northern Reserve Straight Rye Whiskey by Fremont Mishcief Distillery, Seattle, WA

Tom's Foolery Rye Whiskey, Chagrin Falls, OH.

Nelson's Green Brier Tennessee White Whiskey by Nelson's Green Brier Distillery, Nashville, TN.

THE Scotch-Irish immigrant distillers had some exposure to using rye in whiskey production, but for their German immigrant neighbors, rye had been the primary grain used in the production of schnapps and vodka back in northern Europe. They continued this distilling practice, particularly in Pennsylvania and Maryland, where rye whiskey, with its distinctive hard-edged, grainy palate, remained the dominant whiskey type well into the twentieth century.

Rye whiskey was more adversely affected by Prohibition than bourbon was. A generation of consumers weaned on light-bodied and relatively delicate white spirits turned away from pungent, full-bodied straight rye whiskeys. Production of rye whiskey had vanished altogether from the mid-Atlantic states by the 1980s. A handful of modern rye whiskies whiskeys survived by being made by bourbon distilleries in Kentucky and Indiana, where their primary use was for blending to give other whiskeys more character and backbone. Through these dark years, a small but vocal group of rye whiskey enthusiasts continued to champion it, and today both the national distilleries and a number of new craft distillers are again producing their interpretations of this classic American whiskey style.

Washington Rye by Central Standard Craft Distillery, Milwaukee, WI.

BLENDED AMERICAN WHISKEY

Blending whiskeys is an art form unto itself, where whiskeys from a variety of sources are blended together in sub blends that are themselves blended into a master blend. Dozens, and even hundreds, of whiskeys may be used to make one blend.

Murray Hill Club Special Release Blended Bourbon by Jos. A. Magnus & Co. Distillery, Washington, D.C.

BLENDED whiskeys date from the early nineteenth century when the invention of the column still made possible the production of neutral spirits. Distillers blended one or more straight whiskeys (bourbon and rye) with these neutral spirits in varying proportions to create their own branded blend. The taste and quality of these whiskeys, then as now, varies according to the ratio of straight whiskey to neutral grain spirit. Early blends were frequently flavored with everything from sherry to plug tobacco. Compared to straight whiskeys, they were inexpensive and bland. Modern blends utilize dozens of different straight whiskeys to ensure a consistent flavor profile. Blended American whiskeys had a great sales boost during and just after World War II, when distillers promoted them as a way of stretching their limited supply of straight whiskey. Blended whiskeys were considered to be too bland by bourbon and rye drinkers, and consumers with a taste for lighter spirits soon migrated over to vodka and gin.

CORN WHISKEY

True Blue Corn Whiskey, made from Hopi blue corn by Balcones Distilling, Waco, TX.

The Notch Nantucket Island Single Malt Whiskey by Triple Eight Distillery, Nantucket, MA.

Sherry Wood American Single Malt Whiskey by Westland Distillery, Seattle, WA.

CORN whiskey, an unaged, clear spirit, was the first truly American whiskey, and the precursor to bourbon. Scotch-Irish farmers produced it in their stills for family consumption or to trade for store goods. When state and federal excise taxes were permanently introduced during the Civil War, most of the production of corn whiskey went underground to become moonshine, where it has remained ever since. A modest amount of commercial corn whiskey is still produced and consumed in the South, while an increasing number of craft-whiskey distilleries are now experimenting with this more interesting alternative to vodka.

American Cask Strength Single-Malt Whiskey by Moylan's Brewing Co., Novato, CA.

Colkegan Single Malt Whiskey by Santa Fe Spirits, Santa Fe, NM.

CANADIAN WHISKEY

CANADIAN whiskies, as with their American cousins, originated on the farm. These early whiskeys were made primarily from rye, though over time Canadian distillers turned to corn, wheat, and other grains. Canadians continue to refer to their whiskey as rye, even though the mash bill is now predominantly a mix of corn, wheat, and barley. Several of the new generation of Canadian craft distillers and, more recently, national distillers in Ontario and Alberta are, however, now marketing both all-malt and "true" rye whiskeys.

NOT-SO-TRIVIAL PURSUIT

The first waves of British settlers in North America were a thirsty lot. It is recorded that the Pilgrims chose to make final landfall in Massachusetts, even though their original destination was Virginia, primarily because they were almost out of beer.

The first locally made alcoholic beverage was beer, although the limited supply of barley malt was frequently supplemented by everything from spruce tips to pumpkin. Distilled spirits soon followed, with rum made from imported Caribbean molasses dominating in the northern colonies and an assortment of fruit brandies in the South.

THE HISTORY OF NORTH AMERICAN WHISKEY

Whiskey barrels on display in an old truck outside the Jeptha Creed Distillery, Shelbyville, KY.

Flames shoot out of a barrel as it is charred at Canton Cooperage, Lebanon, KY.

Farm distillers are proud of the quality of grain they grow for their whiskeys.

The Code of Federal Regulations (CFR) stipulates that most types of North American whiskeys be aged in new, charred oak barrels.

NORTH American whiskeys are all-grain spirits that have been produced from a mash bill that usually mixes together corn, rye, wheat, barley, and other grains in different proportions, and then is aged for an extended period of time in wooden barrels. These barrels may be new or used, and charred or uncharred on the inside, depending on the type of whiskey being made.

Most non-craft North American whiskeys are made in column stills. The United States government requires that all whiskeys:

Be made from a grain mash.

Be distilled at 90 percent ABV or less.

Be reduced to no more than 62.5 percent ABV (125° proof) before being aged in oak barrels (except for corn whiskey, which does not have to be aged in wood).

Have the aroma, taste, and characteristics that are generally attributed to whiskey.

Be bottled at no less that 40 percent ABV (80° proof).

CLASSIFICATIONS OF NORTH AMERICAN WHISKEYS

NORTH AMERICAN whiskeys are essentially classified by the type or variety of grains in the mash bill, the percentage or proof of alcohol at which they are distilled, and the duration and manner of their aging.

STYLE	DEFINITION	HOWEVER...
Bourbon Whiskey	Must contain a minimum of 51 percent corn, be produced in the United States, be distilled at less than 80 percent ABV (160° proof) and, be aged in new charred barrels. To be straight bourbon whiskey, it must be aged for a minimum of two years.	In practice, virtually all straight whiskeys are aged for at least four years. Any bourbon—or any other domestic or imported whiskey—that is aged less than four years must contain an age statement on the label.
Small Batch Bourbon	Bourbons that are bottled from a small group of specially selected barrels that are blended together.	The choice of barrels is purely subjective on the part of the master blender.
Single Barrel Bourbon	Bourbon from one specific cask.	The choice of the barrel is purely subjective on the part of the master blender.
Tennessee Whiskey	Must be distilled and aged in Tennessee, contain a minimum of 51 percent corn, be distilled at less than 80 percent ABV (160° proof), be filtered through a bed of sugar-maple charcoal, and be aged for a minimum of two years in new charred barrels.	In recent years, as the sales volume of Tennessee whiskeys has increased, the aging on many of the major brands beyond the required minimum of two years has decreased. You have been warned.
Rye Whiskey	Must contain a minimum of 51 percent rye grain, be distilled at less than 80 percent ABV (160° proof), and be aged for a minimum of two years in new charred barrels.	Rye whiskey's dry, peppery, astringent character requires at least four years of aging to soften its otherwise hard edge.
Blended American Whiskey	Must contain at least 20 percent straight whiskey, with the balance being unaged neutral spirit or, in a few cases, high-proof light whiskey.	It has a general whiskey flavor profile (most closely resembling bourbon), but lacks any defining taste characteristic.

A stirring paddle sits over a moonshine wash.

Barley growing in a field in Washington State.

STYLE	DEFINITION	HOWEVER...
Corn Whiskey	This commercial product must contain at least 80 percent corn, be distilled at less than 80 percent ABV (160° proof) and be aged for a minimum of two years in new or used uncharred barrels.	Corn whiskey is the exception to the rule that requires whiskey to be aged to reach its full flavor potential. Well-made corn whiskey has a bright, fruity, almost sweet palate that fades with time.
Moonshine Whiskey (aka white lightning, corn likker, white dog)	Distilled from a mix of corn and sugar and aged in Mason jars and jugs.	It is aged for the length of time that it takes the customers to get home or the Dukes of Hazzard to make a delivery in the *General Lee.*
Canadian Whisky	Made primarily from corn or wheat, with a supplement of rye, barley, or barley malt. There are no Canadian government requirements for the percentages of grains used in the mash bill. They are aged, primarily in used oak barrels, for a minimum of three years, with most brands being aged for four to six years.	Virtually all Canadian whiskies (except the pot-distilled malt whiskies of Glenora in Nova Scotia) are blended from different grain whiskeys of different ages.
Bulk Canadian Whiskies	Usually shipped in barrels to their destination country, where they are bottled. These bulk whiskeys are usually bottled at 40 percent ABV (80° proof) and are usually no more than four years old.	Additional aging statements on the labels of some of these whiskeys should be treated with deep skepticism.
Bottled in Canada Whiskeys	Generally have older whiskeys in their blends and are bottled at 43.4 percent ABV (86.8° proof).	Age, in this context, is still a relative thing. Ten-year-old Canadian whisky is considered a really, really old whiskey.

The Willett Distillery, Bardstown, KY.

Stryker Smoked Single Malt Whiskey by
Andalusia Whiskey Co., Blanco, TX.

NORTH AMERICAN WHISKEY REGIONS

North America's variations of whiskey are as nuanced and distinct as the continent's regions. Most are aged in new wood barrels, but beyond that there has been much experimenting in recent years.

UNITED STATES

Kentucky produces all types of North American whiskeys, except for Tennessee and Canadian. It currently has the largest concentration of whiskey distilleries on the continent, with new facilities, both national and craft, opening every year over the past decade. But it may soon cede that claim to Michigan, Colorado, or one of the Pacific Northwest states as new craft distilleries continue to open.

Tennessee started out as bourbon country, and while its two major national whiskey distilleries specialize in the distinctive Tennessee style of whiskey, a new generation of bourbon craft distilleries have sprung up in the second decade of the 21st century.

Other states such as Indiana and Virginia still have large distilleries that produce straight whiskeys. In recent years, new craft-whiskey distilleries have opened throughout the United States, with noteworthy concentrations in New York, Colorado, California, and the Pacific Northwest.

CANADA

Ontario has the largest concentration of national whiskey distilleries in Canada, with three. Alberta has two, and Manitoba, Quebec and Nova Scotia each have one, producing mostly blended whiskey. Glenora in Nova Scotia and Kittling Ridge in Ontario have lead the new generation of Canadian craft distillers in producing a variety of straight rye and malt whiskeys.

Barrels of bourbon
aging at the Woodford
Reserve Distillery.

REGIONAL FLAVORS

There are now more than 1,200 craft distilleries in most (if not all) 50 states that are producing such standard whiskey styles as bourbon, corn, and rye, as well as many experimental variations. One example is Wasmund's Single Malt Whisky from the Copper Fox Distillery, Virginia. Both its Sperryville and Williamsburg distilleries floor malt their own barley, smoking the grain in various fruit woods for added flavor and complexity. This sort of production twist, which has its roots in craft brewing, is increasingly becoming a distinctive feature

Rick Wasmund malts barley by hand at the Copper Fox Distillery, Sperryville, VA.

Additionally, there are a number of distilling plants, both long established and craft operations, that rectify (redistill), process, and bottle spirits that were originally distilled elsewhere. These distilleries, in addition to sometimes bottling bourbon and rye that has been shipped to them in bulk, may also create their own blended whiskeys. Some of these whiskeys can be relatively inexpensive "well" brands that are sold mainly to taverns and bars for making mixed drinks. But others, particularly from craft distillers and craft spirit marketers, are marketed as high-end, high-priced products. This selling of bulk spirits (both aged and unaged) between distillers is a practice that dates back to the beginning of commercial distilling, and while not much talked about in public, is both legal and an accepted way of doing business in the distillery industry. For example, the largest whiskey distiller in Indiana sells virtually all of its bourbon and rye whiskey production to other whiskey distilleries and marketers.

Wash being made in the mash tun.

Bubbles rise during grain fermentation.

A WHISKEY LEXICON

BONDED WHISKEY is bourbon from a single distillery that was produced in a single "season" and then aged for at least four years in a government-supervised "bonded" warehouse, and bottled at that same facility at 100 proof (50 percent ABV). Distillers originally pushed for this law, passed in 1897, to avoid having to pay the excise tax until the whiskey was aged and ready for market. In a day when rectifiers, in order to make clear spirits taste like whiskey, were liable to adulterate them with any number of illicit and sometimes poisonous flavoring agents, "Bottle in Bond" offered the protection for the consumers and whiskey brands alike. Bonded whiskeys drifted into obscurity for a while, but are returning to popularity as a new generation of craft distillers tries to distinguish their spirits from the products of blending houses.

THE MASH is the mix of crushed grain (including some malt that contains enzymes to break down grain starches into sugars) and hot water from which the distiller draws a liquid extract called wort. The wort is fermented into a simple beer called the wash, which is then distilled.

SOUR MASH is the fermentation process by which a percentage of a previous fermentation is added to a new batch as a "starter" to get the fermentation going and maintain a level of consistency from batch to batch. A sweet mash means that only fresh yeast is added to a new batch to start fermentation.

STRAIGHT WHISKEY is unblended whiskey that has been aged for at least two years and contains no neutral spirit or flavorings. Bourbon, Tennessee, rye, and corn whiskeys can all be straight whiskeys. There is also a spirit, simply called "straight whiskey," that is made from a mixture of grains, none of which accounts for 51 percent of the mash bill.

SCOTCH WHISKY, IRISH WHISKEY, AND OTHER WHISKEYS OF THE WORLD

Whiskey is defined, in its most basic sense, as a spirit that is distilled from grain. Sometimes, the grain has been malted, sometimes not. What distinguishes whiskey from vodka, gin, aquavit, and other grain-based spirits is that it is aged, often for long periods of time, in wooden barrels (usually oak). This barrel aging softens the rough palate of the raw spirit, adding aromatic and flavoring nuances along with the base amber hue that sets whiskeys apart from white grain spirits.

THE HISTORY OF SCOTCH WHISKY

The basis of Scotch whisky is the heather-flavored ales made from barley malt that the Picts and their prehistoric ancestors brewed. Archeologists have found evidence of such brewing dating back to at least 2000 BCE. This ale, still produced today by at least one Scottish microbrewer, was low in alcohol and not very stable.

Starting in the ninth century, Irish monks arrived in Scotland to Christianize their Celtic brethren. They brought along the first primitive stills, which they had picked up during their proselytizing visits to mainland Europe during the Dark Ages. The local Picts soon found that they could create a stable alcoholic beverage by distilling heather ale. Simple stills came to be found in most rural homesteads, and homemade whisky became an integral part of Gaelic culture.

The $187-million new Macallan Distillery in Speyside.

Chivas Brothers Ltd. Tormore Distillery.

As long as Scottish kings ruled the country from Edinburgh, the status quo of whisky as just another farm product was more or less maintained. But the Act of Union in 1707 that combined England, Wales, and Scotland into the United Kingdom altered the Scotch whisky scene forever. The London government soon levied excise taxes on Scottish-made whisky (while at the same time cutting the taxes on English gin). The result was a predictable boom in illicit distilling. In 1790s Edinburgh, it was estimated that more than 400 illegal stills competed with just eight licensed distilleries. A number of present-day Scottish distilleries, particularly in the Highlands, have their origins in such illicit operations.

The Excise Act of 1823 reduced taxes on Scotch whisky tolerably. This act coincided with the dawn of the industrial revolution, and entrepreneurs were soon building new, state-of-the-art distilleries. The local moonshiners (called smugglers) did not go quietly. Some of the first licensed distillers in rural locations were threatened by their illicit peers. But in the end, production efficiencies and the rule of law won out. The whisky that came from these distilleries was made exclusively from malted barley that had been kiln dried over peat fires. The smoke from these peat fires gave the malt a distinctive tang that made the Scottish product instantly identifiable by whiskey drinkers all over the world.

The nineteenth century brought a rush of changes to the Scotch whisky industry. The introduction of column stills early in the 1830s led to the creation of grain whisky, which in turn led to blended Scotch whisky in the late 1860s. The smooth blandness of the grain whisky toned down the assertive smoky character of the malt whiskeys. The resulting blended whisky was milder

Talisker 18-year-old Single Malt Scotch Whisky.

and more acceptable to foreign consumers, particularly the English, who turned to Scotch whisky in the 1870s when a phylloxera infestation (an insect pest that destroys grape vines) in the vineyards of Europe disrupted supplies of cognac and port, two of the mainstays of civilized living. Malt whisky distilleries were bought up by blending companies, and their output was blended with grain whiskeys to create the great blended brands that have come to dominate the market. The malt whisky distilleries took a backseat to these brands and sold most or, in some cases, all of their production to the blenders. The recent popular revival of malt whiskeys has led most of the distilleries to come out with bottlings of their own products.

By the 1990s, international liquor companies owned most of the old-line malt whisky distilleries, a situation that continues to this day. More recently, a new generation of craft-whiskey distilleries have begun production in Great Britain, not only in Scotland, but also in England.

Laphroaig 10-year-old Single Malt Scotch Whisky from the Island of Islay.

WHY BLENDED SCOTCH WHISKY IS A GOOD THING, EVEN IF YOU PREFER SINGLE MALTS

It is a truism of religion that converts frequently become the most zealous of believers. Among freshly minted modern-day enthusiasts of Scotch malt whiskeys, it is a frequently heard refrain that malt whiskeys are superior to the blended article, and that the latter are just not worth bothering with. Personal taste is ultimately subjective, of course. But single-malt drinkers should raise their hats in salute whenever a Dewar's or Johnnie Walker delivery truck drives by, because without these blended brands most of the remaining malt distilleries would not exist. Blended Scotch whiskies require a blend of dozens of different malt whiskeys to be combined with the grain whisky to create the desired blend. The individual percentages of each malt whisky may be small, but each contributes its unique character to the blend. A blender will thus need to buy or produce a large amount of different malt whiskeys to maintain the consistency of the blend. Thus, for a malt whisky distillery, the single malt may get all of the glory, but the blends ultimately pay the bills.

THE HISTORY OF IRISH WHISKEY

The Scots most likely learned about distilling from the Irish (though they are loath to admit it). The Irish in turn learned about it, according to the Irish at least, from missionary monks who arrived in Ireland in the seventh century. The actual details are a bit sketchy for the next 700 years or so, but it does seem that monks in various monasteries were distilling *aqua vitae* ("water of life"), primarily for making medicinal compounds. These first distillates were probably grape or fruit brandy rather than grain spirit. Barley-based whiskey (the word derives from *uisce beatha*, the Gaelic interpretation of *aqua vitae*) first appears in the historical record in the mid-1500s, when the Tudor kings began to consolidate English control in Ireland. Queen Elizabeth I was said to be fond of it and had casks shipped to London regularly.

The imposition of an excise tax in 1661 had the same effect as it did in Scotland, with the immediate commencement of the production of poteen (the Irish version of moonshine). This did not, however, slow the growth of the distilling industry, and by the end of the eighteenth century there were more than 2,000 stills in operation.

Under British rule, Ireland was export-oriented, and Irish distillers produced large quantities of pot-distilled whiskey for export into the expanding British Empire (along with grains and assorted foodstuffs). In the late nineteenth century, more than 400 brands of Irish whiskey were being exported and sold in the United States.

This happy state of affairs lasted into the early twentieth century, when the market began to change. The Irish pot still users were slow to respond to the rise of blended Scotch whisky with its column-distilled, smooth-grain-whisky component. When national Prohibition in the United States closed off their largest export market, many of the smaller distilleries closed. The remaining distilleries then failed to anticipate the coming of repeal (unlike the

Scotch distillers) and were caught short when it came. The Great Depression, trade embargoes between the newly independent Irish Republic and the United Kingdom, and World War II caused further havoc among the distillers.

In 1966, the three remaining distilling companies in the Republic of Ireland—Powers, Jameson, and Cork Distilleries—merged into a single company, Irish Distillers Company (IDC). In 1972, Bushmills, the last distillery in Northern Ireland, joined IDC. In 1975, IDC opened a new mammoth distillery at Midleton near Cork, and all of the other distilleries in the republic were closed down with the production of their brands being transferred to Midleton. For a 14-year period, the Midleton plant and Bushmills in Northern Ireland were the only distilleries in Ireland.

This sad state of affairs ended in 1989, when a potato-peel ethanol plant in Dundalk was converted into a whiskey distillery. The new Cooley Distillery began to produce malt and grain whiskeys, with the first three-year-old bottlings released in 1992. Since then a variety of new national and craft distilleries have opened, or in the case of Tullamore Dew, reopened, in Ireland, with many more being planned.

Distiller Lance Winters leads a group of other distillers on a tour of St. George Spirits/Hangar 1 Vodka. Here, they are marveling at the gleaming column stills.

DISTILLING TIMELINE

Spirit Type	Fermentation	Min. aging	Max. aging
BRANDIES			
Brandy VS	3 weeks	2 years	5 years
Brandy VSOP	3 weeks	4 years	15 years
Brandy XO	3 weeks	6 years	20–30 years
Grappa	1 week	1 month	3 years
Apple Brandy	3 weeks	2 years	20 years
Fruit Brandy	3 weeks	4–6 months	4 years
WHISKEYS			
Scotch	1 week	3 years	30 years
Irish	1 week	3 years	10 years
Bourbon	1 week	2 years	20 years
Tennessee	1 week	2 years	6 years
Rye	1 week	2 years	25 years
Corn	4 days	2 years	2 years
Canadian	1 week	3 years	10 years
Moonshine	4 days	1 week	1 week
RUMS			
White	3 days	2 months	2 years
Golden	3 days	1 year	3 years
Dark	1 week	1 year	4 years
Añejo/Aged	1 week	5 years	30 years
TEQUILAS			
Blanco	1 week	None	2 months
Reposado	1 week	3 months	9 months
Añejo/Aged	1 week	1 year	4 years
VODKAS			
All	3 days	None	3 months
GINS			
Dry	3 days	None	None
Genever	1 week	1 year	3 years

Karuizawa Number One Single Cask Whisky (Japan). The distillery is located in the foothills of Mount Asama, an active volcano.

Yamazaki Distillery Shimamoto, Osaka, Japan 12-year-old Single Malt Whisky (Japan)

THE HISTORY OF JAPANESE WHISKEY

The modern Japanese whiskey industry can trace its beginnings back to one man, Masataka Taketsura. The son of a sake brewer, Taketsura went to Scotland in 1918 and spent two years studying chemistry at Glasgow University and working at a Scotch whisky distillery in Rothes in the Highlands. He returned to Japan in 1920 with a Scottish bride and a determination to change the Japanese distilling industry.

The Japanese were then; as they are now, major consumers of Scotch whisky. Locally produced spirits, however, were limited to the fiery sorghum- or sweet-potato-based shochu, and a handful of dubious "whiskeys" that were little more than neutral spirits colored with caramel. Taketsura convinced the owners of what became the Suntory Company to begin production of barley malt and grain whiskeys based on the Scottish model. These whiskeys, some of which are made from imported peat-smoked Scottish malt,

became very successful in the Japanese market. Other distilleries followed Suntory's lead, and these whiskeys, based on Scotch whisky models (and later bourbon whiskey), soon dominated the market. Modern Japanese distillers (including the Nikka Whisky Distillery, which was founded by Taketsura in 1934) have followed this trend and nowadays produce and market a full range of malt and blended whiskeys. Since around 2005, the first of a new generation of craft distilleries have entered the market, producing mostly malt whiskeys.

STYLE	DEFINITION	HOWEVER ...
Single Malt Scotch Whisky	Malt whisky that has been produced at one distillery. It may be a mix of malt whiskies from different years. The barley malt for Scotch whisky is first dried over fires that have been stoked with dried peat. The peat smoke adds a distinctive smoky tang.	If it contains a mix of whiskies from different years, the age statement on the bottle label gives the age of the youngest spirit in the mix.
Vatted Malt Scotch Whisky	Blend of malt whiskies from different Scottish distilleries.	A higly underrated style, for no good reason. The term blended malt whisky means the same thing.
Scotch Grain Whisky	Made from wheat or corn with a small percentage of barley and barley malt.	Rarely bottled, but well-aged examples can be delicate drams.
Blended Scotch Whisky	Blend of grain whisky and malt whisky.	The ratio of malt whisky to grain whisky in the blend can vary considerably among brands. The number of malt whiskeys in the malt whisky component can range from a handful to dozens
Irish Pot Still Whiskey	Unless labeled as such, Irish whiskeys are a mix of pot- and column-distilled whiskeys.	Once upon a time, all Irish whiskeys were pot-distilled. Column stills were for Scots.
Irish Malt Whiskey	Can be pot-distilled, column-distilled or a mixture of both.	Irish malts have made a welcome comeback in recent years.
Irish Whiskey	A blend of malt and grain whiskeys.	The ratio of malt to grain whiskey can vary widely, which is not necessarily reflected in the price.
Japanese Malt Whisky	Produced in pot stills from lightly peated barley malt.	Broadly modeled on Scottish Highland Malt Whiskies and, in some cases, done very well indeed.
Japanese Whisky	A blend of malt whisky (Japanese or Scotch) and domestically produced grain whisky.	Not to be confused with *shochu*, native Japanese whisky, which is made from rice, sorghum, or barley and is a very different earthy sort of spirit.
New Zealand Single Malt Whisky	Pot-distilled malt whisky.	New Zealand whisky distilleries open and close with the frequency of rugby sports bars, so good luck finding any.
New Zealand Blended Whisky	A mix of domestic malt and grain whiskies.	Occasionally, it may even have some domestically made whiskey in it.
Australian Whisky	All currently produced Australian whiskeys are pot-distilled malt whiskeys.	Tasmania is the center of the new generation of Australian whisky distilling.

THE HISTORY OF NEW ZEALAND AND AUSTRALIAN WHISKIES

Scottish emigrants brought their whiskey-making skills to New Zealand in the 1840s. A thriving whiskey industry soon developed and operated until 1875, when new, excessively high excise taxes and heavy competition from imported British whiskeys forced the local commercial distilleries to shut down. A new, almost commercial-sized moonshine trade quickly replaced them, a situation that continues to this day.

In 1968 a new national whiskey distillery opened in Dunedin, which lasted until 1997. It produced a range of malt and grain whiskeys, broadly in the Scottish style, from locally grown grain. Even the barley malt is kilned and smoked using local peat. Since the beginning of the 21st century, a modest number of new craft whiskey distilleries have begun production.

Australian whiskey production has experienced a similar varied history, with assorted 19th-century producers popping up in the various states, only to be driven out of business by British imports. Early attempts in the 1990s to revive whiskey production have been followed more recently by a new generation of more successful craft-whiskey distillers, particularly on the island of Tasmania.

Limeburners Single Malt Whisky, Cask Strength, Sherry Cask from the Great Southern Distilling Company Albay Australia.

Thousands of barrels stacked outside a cooperage.

THE BASIS OF SCOTCH WHISKY, IRISH WHISKEY, JAPANESE WHISKY, TAIWAN WHISKY, INDIAN AND PAKISTANI WHISKY, NEW ZEALAND AND AUSTRALIAN WHISKIES

All of these whiskey styles, while very different in taste and style, are based on malted barley as the dominant source of flavor and character.

SCOTLAND
There are two basic categories of Scotch whisky: malt whisky, which is made exclusively from malted barley that has been dried over smoking peat fires, and grain whisky, which is made from unmalted wheat or corn. These whiskeys are aged in used wooden bourbon or sherry barrels for a minimum of three years, although five to ten years is the general practice.

IRELAND
There are two basic categories of Irish whiskey: malt whiskey, which is made exclusively from malted barley that has been kiln-dried, but not over peat fires, and grain whiskey, which is made from unmalted wheat or corn. These whiskeys are aged in used wooden bourbon or sherry barrels for a minimum of three years, although five to eight years is the norm.

JAPAN
Japanese whiskeys, both malt and blended, are broadly based on Scotch whiskeys, with some top brands even being made with imported Scottish water and peat-smoked barley malt. The peat-smoke character of Japanese whiskeys is generally more subtle and delicate than their Scottish counterparts. Japanese whiskeys may be aged in both new and used (usually bourbon) wooden barrels, which may be either charred or uncharred.

TAIWAN
Taiwan whiskeys have followed the Japanese model, and are mostly Scottish-style malt whiskeys.

INDIA AND PAKISTAN
Whiskey in India has a long, if rather mixed history, with the popularity of whiskey dating back to the British Raj. However, most of what is sold as whiskey in India (Bagpiper is a major brand), is actually made from sugarcane—so it is technically rum. As a result, it cannot be exported to the European Union, the United States and other countries that have laws and regulations that specifically define whiskey as a grain-based spirit. In the past few years, a small amount of true malt whiskey, broadly in the Scottish style, is being produced, primarily for the export trade. Pakistan, officially a "dry" Muslim country, has one large brewery that also produces malt whiskey—officially only for sale only to non-Muslims.

NEW ZEALAND AND AUSTRALIA
New Zealand and Australian whiskeys both draw on Scottish, Irish, and American traditions in a cheerfully mixed manner, using both peated and unpeated locally-grown barley malt to produce mostly pot-distilled malt whiskeys that are aged in used bourbon and wine barrels for a theoretical, if not always absolute, minimum of six years for malt whiskey.

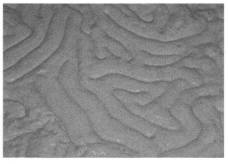

Detail of fermenting barley wash for making whiskey.

The Spirit of Hven Distillery in Sweden experiments with the effects of differents styles of music on the aging process by pumping sound into the barrels where spirits are resting.

THE DISTILLATION OF SCOTCH WHISKY, IRISH WHISKEY, JAPANESE WHISKY, NEW ZEALAND WHISKY, AUSTRALIAN WHISKEY, TAIWAN WHISKY, AND EUROPEAN UNION WHISKEYS

Double- and even triple-distillation is the norm for this family of barley malt–based whiskeys.

SCOTLAND
All Scotch malt whiskeys are double-distilled in pot stills, whereas Scotch grain whiskeys are made in column stills.

IRELAND
Irish whiskeys, both blended and malt, are usually triple distilled through both column and pot stills, although there are a few exclusively pot-distilled brands.

JAPAN, TAIWAN, INDIA, AND PAKISTAN
Japanese whiskeys follow the Scottish tradition, with malt whiskeys being double-distilled in pot stills and grain whiskeys in column stills.

NEW ZEALAND AND AUSTRALIA
Both New Zealand and Australian malt and grain whiskeys are double distilled in pot stills, with some Tasmanian distilleries reportedly experimenting with triple distillation.

SCOTCH WHISKY, IRISH WHISKEY, JAPANESE WHISKY, NEW ZEALAND AND AUSTRALIAN WHISKY REGIONS

SCOTLAND

The Highlands consist of the portion of Scotland north of a line from Dundee on the North Sea coast in the east to Greenock on the Irish Sea in the west, including all of the islands off the mainland except for Islay. Highland malt whiskeys cover a broad spectrum of styles. They are generally considered aromatic, smooth, and medium bodied, with palates that range from lush complexity to floral delicacy. The subregions of the Highlands include Speyside; the North, East, and West Highlands; the Orkney Isles; and the Western Islands (Jura, Mull, and Skye).

The Lowlands encompass the entire Scottish mainland south of the Highlands except the Kintyre Peninsula where Campbeltown is located. Lowland malt whiskeys are light bodied, relatively sweet, and delicate.

Islay is an island off the west coast. Traditional Islay malt whiskeys are intensely smoky and pungent in character with a distinctive iodine or medicinal tang that is said to come from sea salt permeating the local peat that is used to dry the barley malt. Campbeltown is a port located on the tip of the Kintyre Peninsula on the southwest coast that has its own distinctive spicy and salt-tinged malt whiskeys.

Tasmanian sculptor/farmer/distiller Peter Bignell chars used wine barrels for reuse as whiskey casks at Bellgrove Distillery.

IRELAND

A series of corporate consolidations and resulting plant closures left the island with only three distilleries, one in County Antrim at the northern tip of Ulster, and two in the Republic of Ireland to the south. Several new and revived distilleries have recently opened in Dublin and elsewhere, and will begin releasing their own self-produced whiskeys in the mid-2020s.

JAPAN

The whiskey distilleries of Japan are scattered throughout Honshu and Hokkaido, the two main northern islands of Japan, with the malt whiskey distilleries located for the most part in mountainous regions where there are good water supplies.

Oswald 'Ossi' Weidenauer from the Destillerie Weidenauer in Austria.

NEW ZEALAND AND AUSTRALIA

New Zealand's last national whiskey distillery closed in 1997, although its maturing whiskeys continue to be released in the market. Since the turn of the 21st century, a dozen or so new-generation craft distilleries have opened and, in some cases, have already closed. Australia has over 100 distilleries in operation, with at least half of them producing whiskey. The greatest concentration of craft whiskey distilleries is in the island state of Tasmania.

EUROPEAN UNION

France, Germany, Austria, Switzerland, the Netherlands, and most of the Scandinavian countries have a sprinkling of whiskey distilleries, most of them craft distilleries producing malt whiskey and the occasional straight rye. The one noteworthy noncraft whiskey, or at least whiskey-like spirit, in this region is Korn, also known as Kornbran (meaning "grain brandy"), a cereal grain spirit made from rye, wheat, barley, or oats in Northern Germany, some of which is aged for a modest period of time in used oak barrels. It is similar to American corn whiskey, and is reputed to be popular with North Sea fishermen as a phlegm cutter. Historical fun fact: Otto Von Bismarck's father owned a Korn distillery.

WHISKEY COCKTAILS

SAZERAC

In a short glass combine

2 ounces (60 ml) rye whiskey

1 teaspoon (5 g) sugar

Stir to blend, then add

Dash Peychaud's bitters

Dash Angostura bitters

1/2 ounce (15 ml) Pernod

2 ice cubes

Stir to blend. Garnish with lemon twist.

DEPTH CHARGE

Fill a tall glass three-quarters full of beer. Pour 1 1/2 ounces (45 ml) Canadian whisky into a shot glass. Drop the shot glass into the glass of beer and drink them together.

WHISKEY SOUR

Fill a short glass with ice. In a shaker, combine

1 1/2 ounces (45 ml) blended whiskey

1 ounce (30 ml) lemon juice

1 tablespoon (15 g) sugar

Crushed ice (half-full)

Shake and strain into the glass.

MANHATTAN

In a shaker, combine

1 1/2 ounces (45 ml) bourbon

3/4 ounce (23 ml) sweet vermouth

Ice

Stir and strain into a martini (cocktail) glass or a short glass. Garnish with a maraschino cherry.

RUSTY NAIL

Fill a short glass with ice cubes. Add

1 ounce (30 ml) Scotch whisky

1/2 ounce (15 ml) Drambuie liqueur

Stir and serve.

Sazerac Rye Whiskey.

Chapter 4
VODKA

Pipes and rectification columns at Sutherland Distilling Company, Livermore, CA.

" THE RELATIONSHIP BETWEEN A RUSSIAN AND A BOTTLE OF VODKA IS ALMOST MYSTICAL. "
Richard Owen, British scientist and drinking buddy of Charles Darwin

AS the story goes, in 988, the Grand Prince of Kiev (Ukraine) decided it was time for his people to be converted from their pagan ways to one of the monotheistic religions that held sway to the south. First came the Jewish rabbis.

He listened to their arguments, was impressed, but ultimately sent them away after noting that the followers of Judaism did not control any land. Next came the Muslim mullahs. Again, he was impressed, both with their intellectual arguments and the success of Islam as a political and military force. But when he was told that Islam prohibited alcohol, he was dismayed and sent them away. Finally, came the Christian priests, who informed him that not only could good Christians drink alcohol, but also that wine was required for church rituals such as communion. That was good enough for the Grand Prince, and on his command his subjects converted en masse to Christianity.

THE HISTORY OF VODKA

Fremont Mischief Distillery.

Historically, the Slavic peoples of the north and their Scandinavian neighbors took alcoholic drinks very seriously. The extreme cold temperatures of winter inhibited the shipment of wines and beers because these low-proof beverages could freeze during transit. Until the introduction of distilling into Eastern Europe in the 1400s, strong drink was made by fermenting wines, meads and beers, freezing them and then drawing off the alcoholic slush from the frozen water.

The earliest distilled spirit in Eastern Europe was made from mead (honey wine) or beer and was called *perevara*. The word vodka (from the Russian word *voda*, meaning "water") was originally used to describe grain distillates that were used for medicinal purposes. As distilling techniques improved, vodka (*wodka* in Polish) gradually came to be the accepted term for beverage spirit, regardless of its origin.

THE BASIS OF VODKA

Vodka is made by fermenting and then distilling the simple sugars from a mash of pale grain or vegetal matter, which can be potatoes, molasses, beets or a variety, of other plants. Rye is the classic grain for vodka, and most of the best Russian and Polish brands are made exclusively from a rye mash. Swedish and Baltic distillers are partial to wheat mashes, although wheat is also used farther east. Potatoes are looked down on by Russian distillers, but they are held in high esteem by some of their Polish counterparts. Molasses is widely used for inexpensive, mass-produced brands of vodka. American distillers use the full range of base ingredients.

VODKA IN RUSSIA

Russians firmly believe that vodka was created in their land. Commercial production was established by the fourteenth century. In 1540, Czar Ivan the Terrible established the first government vodka monopoly. Distilling licenses were handed out to the boyars (the nobility), all other distilleries were banned, and moonshining became endemic.

Vodka production became an integral part of Russian society. Landowners operated stills on their estates and produced high-quality vodkas that were flavored with everything from acorns to horseradish to mint. The czars maintained test distilleries at their country palaces. In 1780, a scientist at one such distillery invented charcoal filtration to purify vodka.

By the eighteenth and into the nineteenth century, the Russian vodka industry was considered technologically advanced. New stills and production techniques from Western Europe were eagerly imported and utilized. State funding and control of vodka research continued. Under a 1902 law, "Moscow vodka," a clear 40 percent ABV rye vodka without added flavorings and soft "living" (undistilled) water, was established as the benchmark for Russian vodka.

Putting labels over the caps of freshly filled bottles of Prezydent Vodka at Polmos Łódz in Łódz, Poland.

The Soviet Union continued government control of vodka production. All distilleries became government owned, and while the Communist Party apparatchiks continued to enjoy high-quality rye vodka, the proletariat masses had to make do with cheap spirits.

Vodka production in the current Russian Federation has returned to the pre-revolutionary pattern. High-quality brands are again being produced for the new social elite and for export, while the popularly priced brands are still being consumed, well, like *voda*.

VODKA AND THE CLASS SYSTEM

The societal attitude toward cheap spirits meant for the proletariat could be summed up by the curious fact that mass-produced vodka was sold in liter bottles with a nonscrew cap. Once you opened the bottle, it couldn't be resealed. You had to drink it all in one session.

VODKA IN POLAND

The earliest written records of vodka production in Poland date from the 1400s, though some Polish historians claim that it was being produced around the southern city of Krakow at least a century earlier. Originally known as *okowita* (from the Latin *aqua vita*, "water of life"), it was used for a variety of purposes in addition to beverages. A 1534 medical text defined an aftershave lotion as "vodka for washing the chin after shaving." Herbal-infused vodkas were particularly popular as liniments for the aches and pains of life.

In 1546, King Jan Olbracht granted the right to distill and sell spirits to every adult citizen. The Polish aristocracy, taking a cue from their Russian peers, soon lobbied to have this privilege revoked and replaced by a royal decree that reserved to them the right to make vodka.

Commercial vodka distilleries were well established by the eighteenth century. By the mid-nineteenth century, a thriving export trade had developed, with Polish vodkas, particularly those infused with small quantities of fruit spirit, being shipped throughout northern Europe and even into Russia.

With the fall of Communism in the late 1980s, the vodka distilleries soon returned to private ownership. Nowadays, high-quality Polish vodkas are exported throughout the world.

VODKA IN SWEDEN

Vodka production in Sweden, which dates from the fifteenth century, has its origins in the local gunpowder industry, where high-proof spirit (originally called *brännvin*) was used as a component of black powder for muskets. When distilleries were licensed to produce beverage alcohol (primarily spice-flavored aquavit, but also vodka), it was with the understanding that gunpowder makers had first priority over beverage consumers.

Home distilling was long a part of Swedish society. In 1830, there were more than 175,000 registered stills in a country of fewer than three million people. This tradition, in a much diminished and illegal form, still continues to this day. Modern Swedish vodka is produced by the Vin & Sprit state monopoly.

an enterprising liquor salesman in South Carolina started promoting it as "Smirnoff White Whisky—No taste. No smell." Sales boomed and American vodka, after marking time during World War II, was on its way to marketing success. The first popular vodka-based cocktail was a combination of vodka and ginger ale called the Moscow Mule. It was marketed with its own special copper mug, examples of which can still be found on the back shelves of liquor cabinets throughout the United States.

Today, vodka is the dominant white spirit in the United States, helped along by its versatility as a mixer and some very clever advertising campaigns. The most famous of these was the classic double-entendre tagline: "Smirnoff—It leaves you breathless."

VODKA IN THE UNITED STATES

Vodka was first imported into the United States in significant quantities around the turn of the twentieth century. Its market was immigrants from Eastern Europe. After the repeal of Prohibition in 1933, the Heublein Company bought the rights to the Smirnoff brand of vodka from its White Russian émigré owners and relaunched vodka into the U.S. market. Sales languished until

The majority of American craft distillers are vodka producers. They are divided between those who purchase neutral grain spirit (NGS) from a third-party supplier and then rectify it in their own facility, and a relative handful of operations that produce and distill their own wash to make vodka. This is actually a serious challenge for craft distillers with pot stills, because it is difficult to produce a high-proof neutral grain spirit without using a column still.

Charcoal filtration used in making vodka at Colorado Pure Distilling.

The best-known, and best-selling, vodka is Tito's Handmade Vodka from the distillery of the same name in Austin, Texas. Despite its carefully cultivated market image as a "handmade" craft product, the base spirit is NGS (neutral grain spirit) produced, at various times, at ethanol plants and national distilleries in the Midwest. For the record, every other major domestic brand of vodka, and many of the craft brands, too, are made the same way.

DISTILLATION OF VODKA

Vodka is distilled in the manner described in the introductory chapter of this book (see page 24). The choice of pot or column stills does, however, have a fundamental effect on the final character of the vodka. All vodka comes out of the still as a clear, colorless spirit. But vodka from a pot still (the sort used for cognac and Scotch whisky) will contain some of the delicate aromatics, congeners, and flavor elements of the crop from which it was produced. Pot stills are relatively inefficient, and the resulting spirit from the first distillation is usually redistilled (rectified) to increase the proof of the spirit. Vodka from a more efficient column still is usually a neutral, characterless spirit.

Except for a few minor exceptions, vodka is not put into wooden casks or aged for any extensive period of time. It can, however, be flavored or colored with a wide variety of fruits, herbs, and spices.

CLASSIFICATIONS OF VODKA

There are no uniform classifications of vodka. In Poland, vodkas are graded according to their degree of purity: standard (*zwykly*), premium (*wyborowy*) and deluxe (*luksusowy*). In Russia, vodka that is labeled *osobaya* (special) is usually a superior-quality product that can be exported, while *krepkaya* (strong) denotes an overproof vodka of at least 56 percent ABV.

In the United States, domestic vodkas are defined by U.S. government regulation as "neutral spirits, so distilled, or so treated after distillation with charcoal or other materials, as to be without distinctive character, aroma, taste, or color." Because American vodka is, by law, neutral in taste, there are only very subtle distinctions between brands. Many drinkers feel that the only real way of differentiating between them is by alcohol content and price.

Maine Distilleries uses locally sourced potatoes to make its Cold River Vodka.

Prentis Orr, left, and Barry Young, founders of Pennsylvania Pure Distillery, stand in front of a chalkboard diagram that outlines how they make their Boyd & Blair Potato Vodka from scratch in Glenshaw, PA.

The hybrid pot still at Heritage Company in Gig Harbor, WA, with a thumper and two columns can make vodka in one pass.

VODKA REGIONS

EASTERN EUROPE

This is the homeland of vodka production. Every country produces vodka, and most also have local, flavored specialties. Russia, Ukraine, and Belarus produce the full range of vodka types, and they are generally acknowledged to be the leaders in vodka production. Only the better brands, all of which are distilled from rye and wheat, are exported to the West.

Poland produces and exports both grain- and potato-based vodkas. Most of the high-quality brands are produced in pot stills.

The Baltic States of Estonia, Latvia, and Lithuania, along with Finland, produce primarily grain-based vodkas, mostly from wheat.

WESTERN EUROPE

This region has local brands of vodka wherever there are distilleries. The base for these vodkas can vary from grains in northern countries, such as the United Kingdom, Holland, and Germany, to grapes and other fruits in the winemaking regions of France and Italy. Sweden has, in recent decades, developed a substantial export market for its straight and flavored wheat-based vodkas.

Tim Smith of Ogden's Own Distillery hikes into Ogden Canyon to collect spring water from its source and uses it to reduce Five Wives Vodka to proof.

Zubrówka vodka by Polmos Bialystocka is flavored with buffalo grass from the Bialowieza forest in Poland. The vodka has a yellow-green tinge (not shown) from the grass infusion.

Label for Koenig's Famous Idaho Potato Vodka, by the Koenig Distillery and Winery.

NORTH AMERICA

The United States and Canada produce vodkas from almost every substrate that can be distilled including, but not limited to, grains, grapes, apples, potatoes, molasses, sweet potatoes, maple syrup, milk, and honey. Stills that have rectification columns large enough to produce vodka are more expensive and refining a spirit to neutral consumes more energy than other spirits, so making vodka from scratch is costly. Many brands are produced by purchasing neutral spirits in bulk, watering to proof and bottling the distillate. A good way to tell if a vodka is made from scratch is to read the origin statement, usually found on the back of the bottle. If the label says "distilled and bottled by...," then legally the Distilled Spirits Plant (DSP) has to have distilled it. If the origin statement says "Produced by..." or "Bottled by...," then it is reasonable to assume that the vodka was made from neutral spirit purchased in bulk from a large factory distillery.

American vodkas are, by law, neutral spirits, so the distinction between nonflavored brands has traditionally been more a matter of price and perception than taste. In order to distinguish their spirits in the market, a number of craft distillers are now making vodkas that show a little more of the residual aromas and flavors of the base material. Some good examples of this are Jackson Hole Still Works Highwater Vodka (corn and oats), Caledonia Spirits Barr Hill Vodka (Honey), Harvest Spirits Core Vodka (apple), and Central Standard Spirits Wisconsin Rye Vodka.

A number of flavored vodkas are also produced both by the major distillers and by an assortment of craft distillers.

VODKA IN UNEXPECTED PLACES

The Caribbean produces a surprising amount of vodka, all of it from molasses. Most of it is exported for blending and bottling in other countries.

Australia produces (and consumes) vast quantities of molasses-based vodka, but few are exported.

Asia has a smattering of local vodkas, with the best coming from Japan.

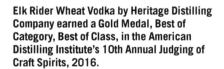

Elk Rider Wheat Vodka by Heritage Distilling Company earned a Gold Medal, Best of Category, Best of Class, in the American Distilling Institute's 10th Annual Judging of Craft Spirits, 2016.

Sagaponacka Wheat Vodka by Sagaponack Farm earned a Double Gold Medal in the American Distilling Institute's 2018 International Judging of Craft Spirits.

VODKA COCKTAILS

SCREWDRIVER
Fill a tall glass with ice. Add

1 1/2 ounces (45 ml) vodka

Orange juice to fill

Stir and serve.

BLOODY MARY
Fill a short glass with ice. Add

1 1/2 ounces (45 ml) vodka

Dash Worcestershire sauce

Dash Tabasco sauce

Dash lemon or lime

Tomato juice to fill

Stir and garnish with celery salt on top.

SEX ON THE BEACH
Fill a tall glass with ice. Add

1 ounce (30 ml) vodka

1 ounce (30 ml) peach liqueur

1 1/2 ounces (45 ml) orange juice

1 1/2 ounces (45 ml) cranberry juice

Stir and serve.

VODKA FLAVORS

As a neutral spirit, vodka lends itself to blending with flavors and fortifying other beverages. In the nineteenth century, high-proof "Russian spirit" was held in high esteem by sherry producers in Spain, who imported it to fortify their wines. Neutral spirits are still used to fortify port, sherry, and other types of fortified wines, although the source of alcohol for such purposes these days tends to be the vast "wine lake" that has been created by European Union agricultural practices.

Flavored vodkas were originally used to mask the flavor of the first primitive vodkas, but they were later considered a mark of the distiller's skill. The Russians and Poles, in particular, still market dozens of flavors. Some of the better-known types are

Off the Hoof Scrapple Flavored Vodka by Painted Stave Distilling, Smyrna, DE.

KUBANSKAYA
Vodka flavored with an infusion of dried lemon and orange peels.

LIMONNAYA
Lemon-flavored vodka, usually with a touch of sugar added.

OKHOTNICHYA
"Hunter's" vodka is flavored with a mix of ginger, cloves, lemon peel, coffee, anise, and other herbs and spices. It is then blended with sugar and a touch of a wine similar to white port. It is a most unusual vodka.

PERTSOVKA
Pepper-flavored vodka, made with both black peppercorns and red chili peppers Starka: "Old" vodka, a holdover from the early centuries of vodka production, which can be infused with everything from fruit tree leaves to brandy, port, Malaga wine, and dried fruit. Some brands are aged in oak casks.

ZUBRÓWKA
A Polish vodka flavored with buffalo (or more properly "bison") grass, an aromatic grass favored by herds of the rare European bison.

In recent years, numerous flavored vodkas have been launched on the world market. The most successful of these have been fruit flavors, such as currant and orange.

THE BIGGEST-SELLING SPIRIT IN THE WORLD THAT YOU HAVE NEVER HEARD OF

Kweichow Moutai, is a variety of baiju from China.

In early 1935, during the Chinese Civil War between the Communist Red Army and Nationalist Kuomintang (KMT), retreating Red Army units on what became known as the Long March, paused in the city of Maotai in the south-central province of Guizhou. The KMT Air Force had been bombing and strafing the Red Army without pause for weeks, but it suddenly stopped this assault when the troops entered the town, and did not renew the attack until the Red Army had left Maotai and moved on. In turn, the Communist forces left the town untouched. The reason for this unofficial truce was that the town of Maotai was the home the distilleries making mao tai, a type of spirit called baijiu that was held in high regard by both sides in the civil war. Politics is one thing, but the possible loss, to both Communists and Nationalists, of what most people in China agreed was the country's finest spirit, was inconceivable and unacceptable.

Mao tai is probably the best known (or more probably the only known) Chinese spirit outside of China. But it is by no means the only variety of baijiu, which is made pretty much everywhere in China where grain is grown. In simple terms, mao tai is to baijiu in China what Cognac is to brandy in France: the most famous type of a wide range of spirits. Baijiu, which literally means "white alcohol" or liquor, is a distilled spirit made primarily from sorghum or wheat mash, although virtually every other sort of cultivated grain including millet, barley, corn, and even rice can also be utilized.

Alcohol production in what is now China dates back far into Neolithic times (at least 7000 BC), with a variety of simple beers and fruit wines being produced. But unlike the ancient Middle East and Europe, where low-alcohol fermented grain beverages and wines were often a substitute for polluted water, the Chinese also had tea, made using boiled water that was safe to drink. This alternative source of a safe, daily beverage allowed the governments of the early kingdoms, and later the national dynasties, to control and tax alcohol products. Alcoholic beverages, if not quite a luxury, were at least not a necessity for healthy living.

A series of tubs contain qu fermentations used in the making of baiju at the VINN Distillery, in Wilsonville, OR.

Fermenting grain beverages usually first requires a process called mashing, by which the starch molecules in crushed grain are converted using enzymes into simple sugars that yeast can feed on to create alcohol and carbon dioxide. In the Middle East and Europe, a process called malting, in which grain (usually barley) was moistened, allowed to partially sprout, which activated natural enzymes in the kernel and then dried to stop the growth of the seed, was used to mash raw grain prior to fermentation.

In China, starting around AD 200, Chinese winemakers (both fermented grain and fruit beverages were collectively known as "wine") created their own distinctive combination mashing and fermentation process using an invention called qu (pronounced like chew). Qu is basically a clump of mashed grains that is stored in a warm, moist, controlled environment for a period of time, which encourages the growth of yeasts and various types of bacteria. The finished qu is then pressed into a brick-shaped mass, and stored until use. Crumbled qu is then added to a grain mash to convert the starches into sugars and also ferment the mash to create alcohol. Qu from each producer is unique, drawing on the local microflora and fauna from the local terroir to create a more sophisticated and complex fermented drink known in the heart of China as huangjiu. In its various versions, huangjiu, which has a look and taste broadly similar to dry sherry, was the drink of choice for the ruling class for the next thousand years, and is still produced to this day. What is frequently translated as "rice wine" on menus in China is usually a type of huangjiu.

The art of distilling was introduced to China from the Islamic world during the Mongolian Yuan Dynasty in the 13th century. The first distilled spirits were probably fruit brandies. But distilling fermenting grain mashes soon followed, and baijiu was born. It was less expensive to make and had a higher alcohol content than the aristocratic huangjiu, and thus quickly became popular throughout the empire. Virtually every town and city had its own baijiu distilleries, most of them small and catering to the local market in a manner similar to medieval alehouses in Europe.

Modern baijiu production dates from the turn of the 20th century. As the creaky Qing Dynasty staggered toward its final collapse in 1912, some of the larger baijiu distillers began looking at distilling techniques abroad. But the political turmoil and foreign invasions during the first half of the century limited the technical advancement, if not necessarily the growth of the baijiu distilling industry. The establishment of the People's Republic of China in 1949, and its fetish-like obsession with industrial modernization, did slowly reach into the baijiu distilling industry. Modern distilleries were built, particularly in the post-Mao era, as private enterprises were encouraged by the new market-oriented regime. By the turn of the 21st century, it has been estimated that there were over 25,000 baijiu distilleries in operation. That number has diminished somewhat in recent years. But there are still a lot of baijiu distilleries in China.

SO, HOW DOES IT TASTE?
Well, to non-Chinese palates, baijiu tends to be an acquired taste. Many inexpensive and even some pricier brands of baijiu can be raw, minimally aged spirits, with a palate similar to high-proof white rum or grappa. Many baijiu stills are very simple alembic-style pot stills that carry over congener-heavy heads, hearts, and tails of the spirit with minimal refinement. There are higher-grade versions that are aged for up to 10 years or more and priced like top-shelf Scotch whiskeys.

But baijiu is not categorized by age, but rather aroma. The four primary categories are strong aroma, sauce aroma, light arom, and rice aroma. Under these general headings there are many, many subcategories, including, phoenix aroma, sesame aroma, medicine aroma, and chi aroma (named after a type of bean curd sauce), to name but a few.

ELSEWHERE IN ASIA
Baijiu is by no means the only spirit endemic to Eastern Aria. Japan has shochu, which is made from buckwheat, rice, or barley; while Korea has a similar spirit called soju. Rice spirits include ruqu de in Vietnam and lao khao in Thailand, while arrack from Indonesia and the Indian subcontinent, made from the sap of unopened coconut flowers, made its way to 18th-century England and Holland as the traditional base for alcoholic punch.

Chapter 5
GIN

Farallon Gin Works Gin Farallon earned a gold medal in the American Distilling Institute's 2017 Judging of Craft Spirits.

" THE PROPER UNION OF GIN AND VERMOUTH IS A GREAT AND SUDDEN GLORY; IT IS ONE OF THE HAPPIEST MARRIAGES ON EARTH, AND ONE OF THE SHORTEST LIVED. "
Bernard DeVoto, American essayist and drinks philosopher

GIN is a juniper berry–flavored grain spirit. The word is an English shortening of *Genever*, the Dutch word for juniper. The origins of gin are a bit murky. In the late 1580s, a juniper-flavored spirit of some sort was found in Holland by British troops who were fighting against the Spanish in the Dutch War of Independence. They gratefully drank it to give them what they soon came to call "Dutch courage" in battle. The Dutch themselves were encouraged by their government to favor such grain spirits over imported wine and brandy by a lack of excise taxes on local drinks.

THE HISTORY OF GIN

Michael Lowe founded New Columbia Distillers, the oldest distillery in Washington, DC, and makers Green Hat Gin.

Gin Lane by William Hogarth

In the 1600s, a Dr. Franciscus de la Boë in the university town of Leiden created a juniper- and spice-flavored medicinal spirit that he promoted as a diuretic. This tonic, called Genever, soon found favor across the English Channel, first as a medicine (Samuel Pepys wrote in 1660 of curing a case of "colic" with a dose of "strong water made with juniper") and then as a beverage.

When the Dutch Protestant William of Orange became king of England in 1689, he moved to discourage the importation of brandy from the Catholic winemaking countries by setting high tariffs. As a replacement, he promoted the production of grain spirits ("corn brandy," as it was known at the time) by abolishing taxes and licensing fees for the manufacture of such local products as gin. History has shown that prohibition never works, but unfettered production of alcohol has its problems, too. By the 1720s, it was estimated that a quarter of the houses in London were used for the production or sale of gin. Mass drunkenness became a serious problem. The cartoonist William Hogarth's famous depiction of such behavior in Gin Lane shows a sign above a gin shop that states, "Drunk for a penny/Dead drunk for two pence/Clean straw for Nothing." Panicky attempts by the government to prohibit gin production,

such as the Gin Act of 1736, resulted in massive illicit distilling and the cynical marketing of "medicinal" spirits with such fanciful names as Cuckold's Comfort and My Lady's Eye Water.

A combination of reimposed government controls, the growth of high-quality commercial gin distillers, the increasing popularity of imported rum and a general feeling of public exhaustion gradually brought this mass hysteria under control, although the problems caused by the combination of cheap gin and extreme poverty extended well into the nineteenth century. Fagin's irritable comment to a child in the film *Oliver*—"Shut up and drink your gin!"—had a basis in historical fact.

Battle Standard Gin by KO Distilling, Manassas, VA.

Bols Barrel Aged Genver by Lucas Bols, Amsterdam, Holland.

Wherever the British Empire went, English-style gins followed. In British colonies in North America, such celebrated Americans as Paul Revere and George Washington were notably fond of gin, and the Quakers were well known for their habit of drinking gin toddies after funerals.

The mid-nineteenth century ushered in a low-key rehabilitation of gin's reputation in England. The harsh, sweetened "Old Tom" style of gin of the early 1700s slowly gave way to a new, cleaner style called dry gin. This style of gin became identified with the city of London to the extent that "London dry" became a generic term for the style, regardless of where it was actually produced.

Genteel middle-class ladies sipped their sloe gin (gin flavored with sloe berries) while consulting *Mrs. Beeton's Book of Household Management* (a wildly popular Victorian cross between the *Joy of Cooking* and Martha Stewart lifestyle books) for gin-based mixed drink recipes. The British military, particularly the officer corps, became a hotbed of gin consumption. Hundreds of gin-based mixed drinks were invented and the mastery of their making was considered a part of a young officer's training. The best known of these cocktails, the gin and tonic, was created as a way for Englishmen in tropical colonies to take their daily dose of quinine, a very bitter medicine, to ward off malaria. (Modern tonic water still contains quinine, though as a flavoring rather than a medicine.)

THE BASIS OF GIN

In Holland, the production of Genever was quickly integrated into the vast Dutch trading system. Rotterdam became the center of Genever distilling as distilleries opened there to take advantage of the abundance of spices that were arriving from the Dutch colonies in the East Indies (present-day Indonesia). Many of today's leading Dutch Genever distillers can trace their origins back to the sixteenth and seventeenth centuries. Examples include such firms as Bols (founded 1575) and de Kuyper (1695).

Belgium developed its own juniper-flavored spirit, called jenever (with a j), in a manner similar to that in Holland (which controlled Belgium for a time in the early nineteenth century). The two German invasions of Belgium in World Wars I and II had a particularly hard effect on jenever producers, as the occupying Germans stripped the distilleries of their copper stills and piping to use in the production of shell casings. The present-day remaining handful of Belgian jenever distillers produce primarily for the local domestic market.

Cheeky packaging for Ableforth's Bathtub Gin pokes fun at gin's sketchy past while producing an award-winning Sloe Gin, formerly a genteel ladies' drink.

BATHTUB GIN

Gin production in the United States dates back to Colonial times, when the Dutch population in New York (originally New Amsterdam) operated gin distilleries as early as the mid-17th century. But the great boost to American gin production was the advent of national Prohibition in 1920. Moonshining quickly moved in to fill the gap left by the shutdown of commercial distilleries. But the furtive nature of illicit distilling worked against the production of the then dominant whiskeys, all of which required some aging in oak casks. Bootleggers were not in a position to store and age illegal whiskey, and the caramel-colored, prune juice–dosed grain alcohol substitutes were generally considered to be vile.

Gin, on the other hand, required no aging, and it was relatively easy to make by mixing raw alcohol with juniper berry extract and other flavorings and spices in a large container such as a bathtub (thus the origin of the term bathtub gin). These gins were generally of poor quality and taste, a fact that gave rise to the popularity of cocktails, in which the mixers served to disguise the taste of the base gin. The repeal of Prohibition at the end of 1933 ended the production of bootleg gin, but gin remains a part of the American beverage scene. It was the dominant white spirit in the United States until the rise of vodka in the 1960s. It remains popular, helped along recently by the revived popularity of the martini and the rise of craft distilleries, where the need for products that can be produced for immediate sale has given rise to many experimental botanical blends to flavor craft gins.

Gin by Corsair Artisan earned a Best of Category Gold medal at the American Distilling Institute's 9th Annual Judging of Craft American Spirits.

Gin may have originated in Holland and developed into its most popular style in England, but its most enthusiastic modern-day consumers are to be found in Spain, which has the highest per capita consumption in the world. Production of London dry–style gin began in the 1930s, but serious consumption did not begin until the mix of gin and cola became inexplicably popular in the 1960s.

Gin and its Dutch cousin genever (jenever in Belgium) are white spirits that are flavored with juniper berries and so-called botanicals (a varied assortment of herbs and spices). The spirit base of gin is primarily grain (usually wheat or rye), which results in a light-bodied spirit. Genever is made primarily from "malt wine" (a mixture of malted barley, wheat, corn, and rye), which produces a fuller-bodied spirit similar to malt whiskey. A small number of Genevers in Holland and Belgium are distilled directly from fermented juniper berries, which produces an intensely flavored spirit.

The chief flavoring agent in both gin and genever is the highly aromatic blue-green berry of the juniper, a low-slung evergreen bush (genus *Juniperus*) that is commercially grown in northern Italy, Croatia, the United States, and Canada. Additional botanicals can include anise, angelica root, cinnamon, orange peel, coriander, and cassia bark. All gin and genever makers have their own secret combination of botanicals, the number of which can range from as few as four to as many as fifteen.

Martin Ryan Distilling Co., Portland, OR, keeps samples of every batch of Aria Gin the distillery has released. They refer back to these bottles when making a new batch.

Wild-foraged botanicals from the California coastal mountains are dried in preparation for making gin at Ventura Spirits.

THE DISTILLATION OF GIN

The base spirit for most non-genever style gin is initially distilled in efficient column stills. The resulting spirit is high proof, light-bodied, and clean, with a minimal amount of congeners (flavor compounds) and flavoring agents. Genever is distilled in less-efficient pot stills, which results in a lower-proof, more flavorful spirit.

Low-quality "compound" gins are made by simply mixing the base spirit with juniper and botanical extracts. Mass-market gins are produced by soaking juniper berries and botanicals in the base spirit and then redistilling the mixture.

Top-quality gin and genever are flavored in a unique manner. After one or more distillations, the base spirit is redistilled one last time. During this final distillation, the alcohol vapor wafts through a chamber in which the dried juniper berries and botanicals are suspended. The vapor gently extracts aromatic and flavoring oils and compounds from the berries and spices as it travels through the chamber on its way to the condenser. The resulting flavored spirit has a noticeable degree of complexity.

No. 209 Chardonnay Barrel Reserve Gin.

Two James Distillery Barrel Reserve Old Cockney Gin.

STYLE	DEFINITION	HOWEVER...
London Dry Gin	The dominant English style of gin in the United Kingdom, former British colonies, the United States and Spain.	It need not be truly "dry" and it lends itself well to mixing.
Plymouth Gin	Relatively full-bodied (compared to London dry gin). It is clear, slightly fruity, and very aromatic.	Originally the local gin style of Plymouth, England, modern Plymouth gin is made only by one distillery in Plymouth, Coates & Co., which also controls the rights to the name Plymouth Gin.
Old Tom Gin	The last remaining example of the original, lightly sweetened gins that were popular in eighteenth-century England.	Limited quantities of Old Tom–style gin are still made by a few British distillers and several American craft distillers, but it is, at best, a curiosity item.
Genever or Hollands	The Dutch style of gin, distilled from a malted grain mash similar to that used for whiskey. Oude (old) Genever is the original style. It is straw-hued, relatively sweet, and aromatic. Jonge (young) Genever has a drier palate and lighter body. Some Genever is aged for one to three years in oak casks. Genever tends to be lower proof than English gin (72 to 80 proof is typical). They are usually served straight up and chilled.	The classic accompaniment to a shot of genever is a dried green herring. Genever is traditionally sold in a cylindrical stoneware crock. Genever-style gins are produced in Holland, Belgium, Germany, and the United States.

Hernö Old Tom Gin earned a gold medal and best of category in the American Distilling Institute's 2017 Judging of Craft Spirits.

Tad Seestedt of Ransom Spirits released Ransom Old Tom Gin, which was the first of the US-made barrel-aged gins, setting of trend that has reverberated through the distilled spirits community.

DON'T CALL IT BARREL AGED!

With the 2008 release of Citadelle Reserve Gin from France, and Ransom Old Tom Gin from Oregon, the gin flavor spectrum swung in a new direction—barrel-aged gins. After reading historical accounts of shipping gin in past centuries using wooden casks, these producers began to experiment with the effects that exposure to wood would have on gin. The cocktail culture swallowed these spirits up with glee, and soon the rush was on. Craft distilleries—many of whom were making gin to have cash flow while waiting for whiskey to age—saw a line extension in these lightly aged spirits. The flavors range anywhere from a classic gin to a juniper-flavored whiskey, depending on what kind of cask was used and how long the spirit rested in it.

There was only one small problem: There are regulations prohibiting putting the words "barrel aged" on beverage alcohol labels. After approving a few barrel-aged gins, the U.S. government revoked some of these labels and declined further applications. This did not stop the products from coming, distillers just had to think of another term. There is an abundance of very interesting gins that are now termed; oak-finished, oak-rested, barrel-rested, reserve, cask-finished, antique,... etc. All of these terms mean one thing: that the gin was barrel aged.

THE COLORFUL ORIGINS OF OLD TOM GIN

The name of Old Tom Gin comes from what may be the first example of a beverage vending machine. In the 1700s, some pubs in England had a wooden plaque shaped like a black cat (an "Old Tom") mounted on the outside wall. Thirsty passersby would deposit a penny in the cat's mouth and place their lips around a small tube between the cat's paws. The bartender inside would then pour a shot of gin through the tube and into the customer's waiting mouth.

GIN
REGIONS

EUROPE

The United Kingdom produces mostly dry gin, primarily from column stills. British gins tend to be high proof (90° proof or 45 percent ABV) and citrus-accented from the use of dried lemon and Seville orange peels in the mix of botanicals. British gins are usually combined into mixed drinks.

Holland and Belgium produce genever, mostly from pot stills. Genevers are distilled at lower proof levels than English gins and are generally fuller in body. Many of these gins are aged for one to three years in oak casks. Some genever producers now market fruit-flavored genever, the best known being black currant. Dutch and Belgian genever are usually chilled and served neat.

Germany produces a genever-style gin called Dornkaat in the North Sea coast region of Frisia. This spirit is lighter in body and more delicate in flavor than both Dutch genever and English dry gin. German gin is usually served straight up and cold.

Spain produces a substantial amount of gin, all of it in the London dry style from column stills. Most of it is sold for mixing with cola.

Boomsma Oude Fine Old Genever, Leeuwarden, Holland.

Elk Rider Crisp Gin by Heritage
Distilling Company earned a Gold
Medal, Best of Category, Best of
Class, in the American Distilling
Institute's 10th Annual Judging of
Craft Spirits, 2016.

The menu board in the image reads:

M E...

Vodka | **Rum** | **Gin** | **Whisky** | **Specials**

White Russian $8 | Cucumber Gimlet $8 | Painkiller $8 | | Pomegranate Rosemary $9 | Barnegat Lemonade $8 | Regular Flight $15 | Bloody Mary $16

Moscow Mule $8 | | Mojito | Gin + Tonic $9 | | | Jersey Mule $8 | Premium Flight $1-$12 $2-$18 $3-$24

Autumn Orange $8 | Cucumber Cosmo $8 | Pomegranate mojito $8 | | Gin Buck $9 | Maple Old Fashioned $8 | Jerseyrita $8 | Side Car $12.50

Vodka Gimlet $8 | | The Weekender $8 | Gimlet $9 | honey bee $9 | Bourbon $12.50 | BoxCar $12.50

Smooth Pink Lemonade $8 | Creamsicle $8 | Cable Car $8 | Gin Martini $9 | Old Fashioned $12.50 | Mint Julep $12.50

Cucumber Mule $8 | dirty martini | | Gin Rita $9 | Whiskey Sour $12.50

Indian Summer Breeze $9

Tax included * in price *

Backbar at Jersey Spirits Distillery, Fairfield, NJ.

NORTH AMERICA

The United States is the world's largest gin market. London dry gin accounts for the bulk of domestic gin production, with most of it produced in column stills, although craft-distillery gin is usually made using hybrid pot stills with columns. American dry gins from the national distillers tend to be lower proof (80° proof or 40 percent ABV) and less flavorful than their English counterparts. This rule applies even to brands such as Gordon's and Gilbey's, which originated in England. The best-selling gin in the United States, Seagram's Extra Dry, was originally a dry gin that was aged for three months in used whiskey barrels to give it a pale straw hue, and a distinctive smooth palate that had a hardcore fan base. The color remains, but in recent years the three month aging has been quietly discontinued.

American craft distillers, in an approach analogous to their craft-brewery counterparts with India Pale Ale, are increasingly experimenting with more exotic and assertive botanicals as their flavoring agents.

American craft distilleries have taken to gin in a major way, with such noteworthy examples as Distiller's Gin #6 from North Shore Distillery in Lake Bluff, Illinois, and Rehorst Premium Milwaukee Gin from the Great Lakes Distillery in Milwaukee, Wisconsin.

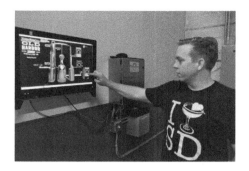

GIN COCKTAILS

CLASSIC MARTINI
In a shaker, combine

2 ounces (60 ml) gin

Dash white vermouth

Ice to fill

Shake and strain and into a martini glass or a short glass. Garnish with an olive.

TOM COLLINS
In a tall glass, combine

2 ounces (60 ml) gin

1 ounce (30 ml) lemon juice

1 tablespoon (15 g) sugar

Stir, and then fill the glass with ice. Fill with club soda.

GIN AND TONIC
Fill a tall glass with ice. Add

1 ½ ounces (45 ml) gin

Tonic water to fill

Garnish with a lime slice.

THE MARTINI AND THE MEANING OF LIFE

The best known of hundreds of gin-based mixed drinks is the gin and white vermouth combination called the martini. As is usually the case with most popular mixed drinks, the origins of the martini are disputed. One school of thought holds that it evolved from the late-nineteenth-century martinez cocktail, a rather cloying mixture of Old Tom–style gin and sweet vermouth. A dissenting sect holds that it was created in the bar of the Knickerbocker Hotel in New York City in the early twentieth century. The ratio of gin to vermouth started out at about two to one, and it has been getting drier ever since. The famed British statesman Winston Churchill, who devoted a great deal of thought and time to drinking, was of the opinion that passing the cork from the vermouth bottle over the glass of gin was sufficient.

Pear-in-bottle brandy.

Chapter 6
BRANDY AND EAU DE VIE

The French-style Charentais still at McMenamins Cornelius Pass Roadhouse (CPR) Distillery.

THE word brandy comes from the Dutch word *brandewijn* (burnt wine), which is how the straightforward Dutch traders who introduced it to northern Europe in the sixteenth century described wine that had been "burnt" or boiled to distill it.

The origins of brandy can be traced back to the growing Muslim Mediterranean states in the seventh and eighth centuries. Alchemists in the region experimented with distilling grapes and other fruits to make medicinal spirits. Their knowledge and techniques soon spread beyond the borders of the territory, with grape brandy production appearing in Spain and probably Ireland (via missionary monks) by the end of the eighth century.

TYPES OF
BRANDY

" NO SIR, CLARET IS THE LIQUOR
FOR BOYS; PORT FOR MEN; BUT
HE WHO ASPIRES TO BE A HERO
MUST DRINK BRANDY. "
Samuel Johnson, eighteenth-century
British writer who loved brandy and
hated whiskey

A bottle of brandy distilled from 100 percent
Viognier wine by Germain-Robin.

Island Orchard Eau de Vie Apple Brandy by Orcas
Island Distillery earned a Gold Medal, Best of
Category, in the American Distilling Institute's
10th Annual Judging of Craft Spirits, 2016.

Pear Brandy by New Deal Distillery earned a Gold
Medal in the American Distilling Institute's 2018
International Judging of Craft Spirits.

Brandy, in its broadest definition, is a spirit
made from fruit juice or fruit pulp and skin.
More specifically, it is broken down into
three basic groupings.

GRAPE BRANDY is brandy distilled from
fermented grape juice or crushed, but not
pressed, grape pulp and skin. This spirit is
aged in wooden casks (usually oak), which
colors it, mellows out the palate, and adds
aromas and flavors.

POMACE BRANDY (Italian grappa and
French marc are the best known examples)
is made from the pressed grape pulp, skins
and stems that remain after the grapes are
crushed and pressed to extract most of the
juice for wine. Pomace brandies, which are
usually minimally aged and seldom see
wood, are an acquired taste. They tend to be
rather raw, although they can offer a fresh,
fruity aroma of the type of grape used, a
characteristic that is lost in regular oak-
aged brandy.

FRUIT BRANDY is the default term for all
brandies that are made from fermenting
fruit other than grapes. (It should not be
confused with fruit-flavored brandy, which
is grape brandy that has been flavored with
the extract of another fruit.)

Fruit brandies, except those made from
berries, are generally distilled from fruit
wines. Berries tend to lack enough sugar to
make a wine with sufficient alcohol for proper
distillation, and thus are soaked (macerated)
in a high-proof spirit to extract their flavor
and aroma. The extract is then distilled once
at a low proof. Calvados, the apple brandy
from the Normandy region of northwestern
France, is probably the best known type of
fruit brandy. *Eau de vie* ("water of life") is a
colorless fruit brandy, particularly from the
Alsace region of France and from California.

BRANDIES BY REGION

FRANCE

French brandy is the catchall designation for brandy produced from grapes grown in other regions. These brandies are usually distilled in column stills and aged in oak casks for varying periods of time. They are frequently blended with wine, grape juice, oak flavorings, and other brandies, including cognac, to smooth out the rough edges. Cognac-like quality designations such as VSOP and Napoleon are often used (see page 107), but they have no legal standing.

The alambic charentais is the most popular style of still for producing Cognac.

COGNAC

Cognac is the best-known type of brandy in the world, a benchmark by which most other brandies are judged. The Cognac region is located on the south-central coast of France, just north of Bordeaux, in the departments of Charente and Charente-Maritime. The region is further subdivided into six growing zones: Grande Champagne, Petite Champagne, Bois Ordinaries, Borderies, Fins Bois, and Bons Bois. The first two of these regions produce the best Cognac and will frequently be so designated on bottle labels. The primary grapes used in making Cognac are the Ugni Blanc, Folle Blanche, and Colombard. The wines made from these grapes are thin, tart and low in alcohol, which are poor characteristics for table wines but perfect for making brandy.

Cognac is double-distilled in specially designed pot stills and then aged in casks made from Limousin or Troncais oak. All Cognacs start out in new oak to mellow the fiery spirit and give them color. Batches chosen for long-term aging are, after a few years, transferred to used, or seasoned, casks that impart less of the oak flavor notes while the brandy matures.

Nearly all Cognacs are a blend of brandies from different vintages and frequently different growing zones. Even those from single vineyards or distilleries have a mix of brandies from different casks. As with champagne, the products of local vineyards are sold to Cognac houses, each of which stores and ages Cognacs from different suppliers. The suppliers then employ master blenders to create and maintain continuity in the house blends drawn from disparate sources.

Park Cognac Single Vineyard Borderies earned a Gold Medal at the American Distilling Institute's 10th Annual Judging of Craft Spirits.

Chateau de Triac Single Vineyard Fins Bois, Cognac.

Alexandre Gabriel, president and owner of Maison Ferrand, evaluates a flight of spirits at the American Distilling Institute's International Judging of Craft Spirits.

Tiffon Cognac XO by Cognac Tiffon earned a Gold Medal in the American Distilling Intitute's 2018 Judging of Craft Spirits.

INDUSTRY STANDARDS FOR COGNAC

Because there are no age or vintage statements on most Cognacs, the industry has adopted some generally accepted terms to differentiate Cognacs. It is important to note that these terms have no legal status, and each Cognac shipper uses them according to his or her own criteria.

VS/VSP/Three Star: (VS: very superior; VSP: very superior pale) A minimum of two years aging in a cask, although the industry average is four to five years

VSOP: (very superior old pale) A minimum of four years' cask aging for the youngest Cognac in the blend, with the industry average between ten and fifteen years

XO/Napoleon: (XO: extra old) A minimum of six years' aging for the youngest Cognac in the blend, with the average age running twenty years or older. All Cognac houses maintain inventories of old vintage Cognacs to use in blending these top-of-the-line brands. The oldest Cognacs are removed from their casks in time and stored in glass demijohns (large jugs) to prevent further loss from evaporation and to limit excessively woody flavor notes.

A distiller stokes a wood fire under the column of an alambic Armagnacais at the Chateau du Tariquet.

Armagnac Castarede Reserve de la Famille, earned a Double Gold Medal in the American Distilling Intitute's 2018 International Judging of Craft Spirits.

Chateau de Maniban V.S.O.P. Bas Armagnac.

HAVE STILL, WILL TRAVEL

Until the 1970s, portable alambic Armagnacais mounted on two-wheel carts were hauled among small vineyards in Armagnac by itinerant distillers called *bouilleurs de cru*. These traveling stills, alas, have mostly given way to larger, fixed in-place setups operated by farmer cooperatives and individual operators.

Christian Drouin, who produces some of the finest Calvados, stands beside a portable still built in 1946 that is now permanently stationed in front of the press room at Domaine Coeur de Lion. It is normally used from February to June. A second still now operates inside the press room.

ARMAGNAC

Armagnac is the oldest type of brandy in France, with documented references to distillation dating back to the early fifteenth century. The Armagnac region is located in the heart of the ancient province of Gascony in the southwest corner of France. As with Cognac, there are regional growing zones: Bas-Armagnac, Haut Armagnac, and Tenareze. The primary grapes used in making Armagnac are also the Ugni Blanc, Folle Blanche, and Colombard. But distillation takes place in the unique alambic Armagnacais, a type of column still that is even less efficient than a typical Cognac pot still. The resulting brandy has a rustic, assertive character and aroma that requires additional cask aging to mellow out and distinguish it from Cognac. The best Armagnac is aged in casks made from the local Monlezun oak. In recent years, Limousin and Troncais oak casks have been added to the mix of casks as suitable Monlezun oak becomes harder to find.

Most Armagnacs are blends, but unlike Cognac, single vintages and single-vineyard bottlings can be found. The categories of Armagnac are generally the same as those of cognac (VS, VSOP, XO, and so on; see sidebar on page 107). Blended Armagnacs frequently have a greater percentage of older vintages in their mix than comparable Cognacs, making them a better value for the discerning buyer.

A variety of Armagnac bottles.

Chateau de Laubade Extra Single Estate Bas Armagnac, 750 ml, earned a Double Gold Medal, Best of Category, Best of Class, in the American Distilling Institute's 10th Annual Judging of Craft Spirits, 2016.

Barreled Grape Immature Brandy by the
Dampfwerk Distillery Co. earned a Gold Medal
in the American Distilling Intitute's 2018
International Judging of Craft Spirits.

BRANDY'S SEASONAL NATURE

Brandy, like rum and tequila, is an agricultural spirit. Unlike grain spirits such as whiskey, vodka, and gin, which are made throughout the year from grain that can be harvested and stored, brandy is dependent on the seasons, the ripening of the base fruit and the production of the wine from which it is made. Types of brandies, originally at least, tended to be location specific. (Cognac, for example, is a town and region in France that gave its name to the local brandy.) Important brandy-making regions, particularly in Europe, further differentiate their local spirits by specifying the types of grapes that can be used and the specific areas (appellation) in which the grapes used for making the base wine can be grown.

AGING TIMELINE

Basic Brandy de Jerez Solera must age for a minimum of six months, Reserva for one year, and Gran Reserva for a minimum of three years.

In practice, the best Reservas and Gran Reservas are frequently aged for twelve to fifteen years. The lush, slightly sweet and fruity notes to be found in Brandy de Jerez come not only from aging in sherry casks but also from the judicious use of fruit-based flavor concentrates and oak essence (boise).

SPAIN
BRANDY DE JEREZ

Brandy de Jerez is made by the sherry houses centered around the city of Jerez de la Frontera in the southwest corner of Spain.

But virtually all Brandy de Jerez is made from wines produced elsewhere in Spain, primarily from the Airen grape in La Mancha and Extremadura, because the local sherry grapes are too valuable to divert into brandy production. Nowadays, most of the distilling is likewise done elsewhere in Spain in column stills. It is then shipped to Jerez for aging in used sherry casks in a solera system similar to that used for sherry wine. A solera is a series of large casks (called butts), each holding a slightly older spirit than the previous one beside it. When brandy is drawn off (racked) from the last butt (no more than a third of the volume is removed), it is replenished with brandy drawn from the next butt all the way down the solera line to the first butt, where newly distilled brandy is added. This system of racking the brandy through a series of casks blends together a variety of vintages (some soleras have more than thirty stages) and results in a speeding up of the maturation process.

PENEDÈS BRANDY

Penedès Brandy is from the Penedès region of Catalonia in the northeast corner of Spain near Barcelona. Modeled after the Cognacs of France and made from a mix of local grapes and the Ugni Blanc of Cognac, it is distilled in pot stills. One of the two local producers (Torres) ages in soleras consisting of butts made from French Limousin oak, whereas the other (Mascaro) ages in the standard non-solera manner, but also in Limousin oak. The resulting brandy is heartier than Cognac, but leaner and drier than Brandy de Jerez.

ITALY

Italy has a long history of brandy production dating back to at least the sixteenth century, but unlike Spain or France, there are no specific brandy-producing regions. Italian brandies are made from regional wine grapes and most are produced in column stills, although there are now a number of small artisanal producers using pot stills. They are aged in oak for a minimum of one to two years, with six to eight years being the industry average. Italian brandies tend to be on the light and delicate side, with a touch of residual sweetness.

GERMANY

German monks were distilling brandy by the fourteenth century, and German distillers had organized their own guild as early as 1588. Yet almost from the start, German brandy (called *Weinbrand*) has been made from imported wine rather than the more valuable local varieties. Most German brandies are produced in pot stills and must be aged for a minimum of six months in oak. Brandies that have been aged in oak for at least one year are called uralt or alter (meaning "older"). The best German brandies are smooth, somewhat lighter than Cognac, and finish with a touch of sweetness.

Siegfried Herzog Destillate specializes in fruit spirits and brandies (below).

SLYRS distillery, Germany (above).

The tasting room at a distillery is a popular stop on the tour. Rick Moersch at the Round Barn Distillery pours some apricot brandy at the tasting room in his winery/brewery/distillery.

UNITED STATES

Grape brandy production in the United States, which until the advent of modern craft distilleries was mostly confined to California, dates back to the Spanish missions in the late eighteenth and early nineteenth centuries. A substantial amount of peach brandy was made by whiskey distillers in southern states prior to Prohibition, however, and apple brandy distilling continued into modern times on a modest scale in New Jersey and Virginia. In the years following the Civil War, brandy became a major industry, with a substantial export trade to Europe by the end of the nineteenth century. For a time, Leland Stanford, founder of Stanford University, was the world's largest brandy producer. Phylloxera and national Prohibition almost shut down the industry in the 1920s.

Repeal started things up again, but as with the bourbon industry, the advent of World War II resulted in brandy producers finding themselves further marking time. Soon after the end of the war, the industry commissioned the University of California at Davis Department of Viticulture and Oenology to develop a prototype "California-style" brandy. It had a clean palate, was lighter in style than most European brandies, and had a flavor profile that made it a good mixer. Starting in the late 1940s, California brandy producers began to change over to this new style.

Apple pulp from the grinder is fed into an accordion-style filter where the juice will be squeezed out to make apple brandy (see page 117) at Laird & Co., North Garden, VA.

High Council Brandy is produced on Cognac-style stills at McMenamins CPR Distillery, in Hilsboro, OR.

Joe and Lesley Heron, founders of Copper & Kings Distillery, produce contemporary brandies in Louisville, KY.

Jepson Old Stock Brandy by Jaxon Keys Winery and Distillery earned a Double Gold Medal, Best of Category, Best of Class, in the American Distilling Institute's 10th Annual Judging of Craft Spirits, 2016.

CONTEMPORARY BRANDIES

Contemporary commercial California grape brandies are made primarily in column stills from table grape varieties such as the Thompson Seedless and Flame Tokay. California brandies are aged for two to twelve years in used American oak (both brandy and bourbon casks) to limit woodiness in the palate, although pot distillers also use French oak. Several California distillers, most notably Korbel, have utilized the Spanish solera method for maturing their brandy. California brandies do not use quality designations such as VSOP or stars. The more expensive brands will usually contain a percentage of older vintages and pot-distilled brandies in the blend.

Craft-distilled brandies, including grape, pomace, and fruit, were the first of the modern generation of craft spirits to enter the U.S. market, starting in California in the late 1980s with producers such as RMS (a venture of Cognac producer Remy Martin), Jepson Vineyards, and the idiosyncratic Santa Cruz winemaker Randall Graham at Bonny Doon Vineyards. From the start, these grape brandy producers generally followed a French-themed muse, with producers such as Germaine-Robin in Mendocino County and Osocalis in the Santa Cruz Mountains going so far as to use the classic Ugni Blanc, Colombard, and Folle Blanche grapes to make their base wine. They installed special Cognac-style pot stills to distill it and then aged their brandies in casks made from imported Limousin or Troncais oak. The resulting brandies, particularly as longer-aged examples come on to the market, have, in some cases, shown levels of complexity and flavor intensity that put them on par with their European counterparts.

Daniel Farber stands next to a new alambic Armagnacais under installation at Osocalis Distillery, Soquel, CA. After distilling for decades on alambic Charentais, Farber is broadening the style of his brandies.

Master distiller and blender Hubert Germain-Robin, left, discusses the qualities of the distillate coming off the still at McMenamins CPR Distillery with Distillery Manager Clark McCool.

Pisco Style Brandy by Leopold Bros.

LATIN AMERICAN
MEXICO
In Mexico a surprising amount of wine is made, but it is little known outside of the country because most of it is used for brandy production. Mexican brandies are made from a mix of grapes, including the Thompson Seedless, Palomino, and Ugni Blanc. Both column and pot stills are used in production, whereas the solera system is generally used for aging. Brandy now outsells tequila and rum in Mexico.

SOUTH AMERICA
South American brandies are generally confined to their domestic markets. The best-known type is pisco, a clear, raw brandy from Peru and Chile that is made from Muscat grapes and double-distilled in pot stills. The resulting brandy has a perfumed fragrance and serves as the base for a variety of mixed drinks, including the famous Pisco Punch.

OTHER REGIONS
Greece produces pot-distilled brandies, many of which, such as the well-known Metaxa, are flavored with Muscat wine, anise, or other spices.

Winemaking in Israel is a well-established tradition dating back thousands of years. But brandy production dates back only to the 1880s, when the French Jewish philanthropist Baron Edmond de Rothschild established what has become the modern Israeli wine industry. Israeli brandy is made in the manner of Cognac from Colombard grapes with distillation in both pot and column stills and maturation in French Limousin oak casks.

In the Caucasus region, along the eastern shore of the Black Sea, the ancient nations of Georgia and Armenia draw on monastic traditions to produce rich, intensely flavored pot-still brandies both from local grapes and from such imported varieties as the Muscadine (from France) and the Sercial and Verdelho (most famously from Madeira).

South Africa has produced brandies since the arrival of the first Dutch settlers in the seventeenth century, but these early spirits from the Cape Colony earned a reputation for being harsh firewater (*witblits*—white lightning—was a typical nickname). The introduction of modern production techniques and government regulations in the early twentieth century gradually led to an improvement in the quality of local brandies. Modern South African brandies are made from Ugni Blanc, Colombard, Chenin Blanc, and Palomino grapes; produced in both pot and column stills, and aged for a minimum of three years in oak.

POMACE BRANDIES

Italy produces a substantial amount of grappa, both the raw, firewater variety and the more elegant, artisanal efforts that are made from one designated grape type and packaged in hand-blown bottles. Both types of grappa can be unaged or aged for a few years in old casks that will tame the hard edge of the spirit without imparting much flavor or color. Marc from France is produced in all of the nation's wine-producing regions, but it is mostly consumed locally. Marc de Gewürztraminer from Alsace is noteworthy because it retains some of the distinctive perfume nose and spicy character of the grape.

Craft pomace brandies from the United States, from producers such as Domaine Charbay in Napa County and Mosby Vineyards in Sonoma, are in the Italian style, and they are usually called grappas, even when they are made from non-Italian grape varieties. This is also true of the pomace brandies from Canada.

GRAPPA: NOT YOUR GRANDPA'S PHLEGM CUTTER

The U.S. government calls it pomace brandy, but ever since immigrants from winemaking countries began arriving in the United States and started to make wine, they were soon refermenting the pressed grape skins from their winemaking and distilling it to make a quick and simple type of brandy. The French call it *marc*, but it is the Italian term *grappa* that has caught on with distillers of every ethnic background.

Craft distillers in the United States have taken to the distilling of grappa from the very start of the industry. Pioneer brandy distillers such as Clear Creek and St. George Spirits have developed specific varietal grappas that are carefully distilled to capture the subtle aromatic notes of the base fruit. These are spirits to delight the nose as much as the taste buds.

Poli Bassano del Grappa, Italy.

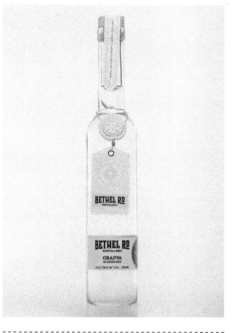

Grappa di Moscato by Bethel Rd. Distillery, Templeton, CA.

APPLE AND OTHER FRUIT BRANDIES

Normandy is one of the few regions in France that does not have a substantial grape wine industry. Instead, it is apple country, with a substantial tradition of hard and sweet ciders that in turn can be distilled into an apple brandy known as Calvados. The local cider apples, which tend to be small and tart, are closer in type to crab apples than to modern table apples. This spirit has its own appellations, with the best brands coming from *Appellation Controlee Pays d'Auge* near the seaport of Deauville, and the rest in ten adjacent regions that are designated *Appellation Reglementee*. *Most Pays d'Auge* and some of the better *Appellation Reglementee* are produced in pot stills. All varieties of Calvados are aged in oak casks for a minimum of two years. Cognac-style quality and age terms such as VSOP and *Hors d'Age* are frequently used on labels but have no legal meaning.

The fruit-growing regions of the upper Rhine River are the prime eau de vie production areas of Europe. The Black Forest region of Bavaria in Germany and Alsace in France are known for their cherry brandies (*kir* in France, *Kirschwasser* in Germany), raspberry brandies (*framboise* and *Himbeergeist*) and pear brandies (poire). Similar eaux de vie are now being produced in the United States in California and Oregon. Some plum brandy is also made in these regions (mirabelle from France is an example), but the best known type of plum brandy is slivovitz, which is made from the small blue sljiva plum throughout Eastern Europe and the Balkans.

Sidetrack Distillery Rasberry Brandy, Kent, WA.

Sebastian Degens of Stone Barn Brandyworks, Portland, OR.

Pot stills at Kymar Farm Winery and Distillery, Charlotteville, NY, where they make an exceptional apple brandy.

Andrew Richards, right, and his father-in-law Rich Kneiper of Shady Knoll Orchards and Distilling, Millbrook, NY, grind apples to make apple brandy.

Slivovitz Plum Brandy by Beaver Pond Distillery, Petersham, MA.

Sunshine Orange Brandy by Stark Spirits, Pasadena, CA.

Island Orchard Eau de Vie Apple Brandy by Orcas Island Distillery.

In the United States, applejack, as apple brandy is called locally, is thought by many to be the first spirit produced in the British colonies. This colonial tradition has continued with Laird's Distillery, established in 1780 in New Jersey as the oldest continuously operating distilling company in the United States with distilleries in New Jersey and Virginia.

Artisan fruit brandy distilling started in California, but in recent years it has spread across the United States, with Calvados-style apple brandies from Clear Creek Distillery in Portland, Oregon, leading the way, while Black Star Farms in Suttons Bay, St. Julian in Paw Paw, and a bevy of other artisan distillers in Michigan and elsewhere have released a wide range of delicate, highly aromatic cherry, raspberry, plum, and other fruit brandies that draw an obvious inspiration from the kirsch and plum brandies of the Black Forest region of southern Germany.

In pre-Prohibition bourbon whiskey distilleries in the South, whiskey distillation was seasonal, and was done after the grain harvest. To fill in the downtime during the summer, many of them also distilled fruit brandies, particularly peach brandy. Today, modern distilling, both national and craft, is an all-year process. But many craft distilleries are now producing both grain spirits and fruit brandies, so, in a sense, this tradition lives on.

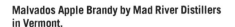

Malvados Apple Brandy by Mad River Distillers in Vermont.

Clear Creek Distillery Apple Brandy Aged 8 Years in French Oak, 750 ml, earned a Gold Medal, Best of Category, in the American Distilling Institute's 10th Annual Judging of Craft Spirits, 2016.

BRANDY COCKTAILS

SIDECAR
Fill a short glass with ice.
In a shaker, combine

1 ounce (30 ml) brandy

1 ounce (30 ml) Triple Sec

1 ounce (30 ml) lemon juice

Ice to fill

Shake and strain into the glass.

STINGER
Fill a short glass with ice. Add

1 ounce (30 ml) brandy

1 ounce (30 ml) white crème de menthe

Stir and serve.

BRANDY ALEXANDER
In a shaker, combine

1 ounce (30 ml) brandy

1 ounce (30 ml) dark crème de cacao

1 ounce (30 ml) cream

Ice to fill

Shake and strain into a large brandy snifter. Dust with nutmeg.

Chapter 7
RUM

Bottles of rum of different ages (youngest to oldest, left to right) at Celebration Distillation in New Orleans.

GRAPES and grain may be the two major raw materials for distillation, but they are by no means the only ones. Sugarcane provides two different fermentables: sugarcane juice and molasses, which is a by-product of sugar refining. Both are used as the basis of rum production, which, as a spirit, ranges across the color and taste spectrum from the almost vodka-like blancos of Puerto Rico to the hearty, deep-hued demeraras of Guyana, with some very distinctive variations in between.

THE HISTORY OF RUM

Sugarcane field, Louisiana.

The history of rum is the history of sugar. Sugar is a sweet crystalline carbohydrate that occurs naturally in a variety of plants. One of those is the sugarcane (*Saccharum officinarum*), a tall, thick grass that has its origins in the islands of present-day Indonesia in the East Indies. Chinese traders spread its cultivation to Asia and on to India. Arabs in turn brought it to the Middle East and North Africa, where it came to the attention of Europeans during the Crusades in the eleventh century.

As the Spanish and Portuguese began to venture out into the Atlantic Ocean, they planted sugarcane in the Canary and Azores Islands. In 1493, Christopher Columbus picked up cane cuttings from the Canaries while on his second voyage to the Americas and transplanted them to Hispaniola, the Caribbean island now shared by Haiti and the Dominican Republic. Portuguese explorers soon did likewise in Brazil.

The Caribbean basin proved to have an ideal climate for growing sugarcane, and sugar production quickly spread around the islands. The insatiable demand in Europe for sugar soon led to the establishment of hundreds of sugarcane plantations and mills in the various English, Spanish, French, Portuguese, and Dutch colonies. These mills crushed the harvested cane and extracted the juice. Boiling this juice caused chunks of crystallized sugar to form. The remaining unsolidified juice was called *melazas* (from the Spanish word for honey, miel); in English this became the word molasses.

Molasses is a sticky syrup that still contains a significant amount of sugar. Sugar mill operators soon noticed that when it was mixed with water and left out in the sun, it fermented. By the 1650s, this former waste product was being distilled into a spirit. In the English colonies, it was called Kill Devil (from its tendency to cause a nasty hangover or its perceived medicinal power, take your choice) or rumbullion (origin uncertain), which was shortened over the years to our modern word rum. The French render this word as *rhum*, while the Spanish call it *ron*.

Rum was used as a cure-all for many of the aches and pains that afflicted those living in the tropics. Sugar plantation owners sold it, at discounted prices, to naval ships that were on station in the Caribbean in order to encourage their presence in local waters and thus discourage marauding pirates.

This naval-rum connection introduced rum to the outside world, and by the late seventeenth century a thriving export trade developed. The British islands shipped rum to Great Britain (where it was mixed into rum punches and replaced gin as the dominant spirit in the eighteenth century) and to the British colonies in North America, where it became very popular. This export of rum to North America, in exchange for New England lumber and dried cod (still a culinary staple in the Caribbean), soon changed over to the export of molasses to distilleries in New England. This was done to avoid laws from the British Parliament, which protected British distillers by forbidding the trade in spirits directly between colonies. This law was, at best, honored in the breach, and smuggling soon became rampant.

The shipping of molasses to make rum in New England distilleries became part of the infamous "slavery triangle." The first leg was the shipment of molasses to New England to make rum. The second leg was the shipment of rum to the ports of West Africa to trade for slaves. The final leg was the passage of slave ships to the sugar plantations of the Caribbean and South America, where many of the slaves were put to work in the sugarcane fields.

The disruption of trade caused by the American Revolution and the rise of whiskey production in North America resulted in the gradual decline of rum's dominance as the American national tipple. Rum production in the United States slowly declined through the nineteenth century, with the last New England rum distilleries closing at the advent of Prohibition in 1920. The famed rumrunners of the Prohibition era were smuggling primarily whiskey into the United States.

In Europe, the invention of sugar extraction from the sugar beet lessened the demand for Caribbean sugar, reducing the amount of molasses being produced and the resulting amount of rum being distilled. Many small plantations and their stills were closed. Rum production receded, for the most part, to countries where sugarcane was grown. The modern history of rum owes a lot to the spread of air-conditioning and the growth of tourism. In the second half of the twentieth century, modern air-conditioning made it possible for large numbers of people to migrate to warm-weather regions where rum remained the dominant spirit. Additionally, the explosive increase in the number of North American and European tourists into rum-drinking regions led to a steady increase in the popularity of rum-based mixed drinks. Nowadays, white rum gives vodka serious competition as the mixer of choice in a number of distinctively nontropical markets.

Manulele Distillers KoHana Koho Hawaiian Agricole Rum.

Cane Land Distilling Co. Rhum Agricole LA Rum.

Malahat Spirits Cabernet Barrel Rum earned a Gold Medal, Best of Category and Best of Class in the American Distilling Institute's 10th Annual Judging of Craft Spirits, 2016.

Aged rum is gaining new standing among consumers of single-malt Scotch, Cognac, and small-batch bourbon, who are learning to appreciate the subtle complexities of this rum. The pot-still rums of Guyana and Jamaica have a particular appeal for Scotch drinkers. (It is no accident that the Scottish whisky merchant and bottler Cadenhead also ages and bottles demerara rum.) The subtle and complex *rhums* of Martinique and Guadeloupe mirror the flavor profiles of the top French brandies in Cognac and Armagnac.

Stark Spirits California Gold Rum.

Bob Ryan and partner Dave Wood at Ryan & Wood Distilleries in Gloucester, Massachusetts.

Diablo's Shadow Navy Strength Rum by Sutherland Distilling Co.

Coaster for Ragged Mountain Rum by Berkshire Mountain Distillers: "Think Globally, Drink Locally"

STYLE	DEFINITION
White Rums	Generally light bodied (although there are a few heavy-bodied white rums in the French islands). They are usually clear and have a very subtle flavor profile. If they are aged in oak casks to create a smooth palate, they are then usually filtered to remove any color. White rums are primarily used as mixers and blend particularly well with fruit flavors.
Golden Rums	Also known as amber rums, these are generally medium bodied. Most have spent several years aging in oak casks, which give them smooth, mellow palates.
Dark Rums	Traditionally, full-bodied, rich caramel-dominated rums, the best are produced mostly from pot stills and frequently aged in oak casks for extended periods. The richest of these rums are consumed straight up.
Spiced Rums	White, golden, or dark rums, they are infused with spices or fruit flavors. Rum punches (such as Planter's Punch) are blends of rum and fruit juices that are very popular in the Caribbean.
Age-Dated Blended Rums	These are aged rums from different vintages or batches that are mixed together to ensure a continuity of flavor in brands of rum from year to year. Some aged rums will give age statements stating the youngest rum in the blend (e.g., a 10-year-old rum contains a blend of rums that are at least 10 years old). A small number of French island rums are vintage dated.

Twenty Boat Amber Rum by South Hollow Spirits, 750 ml, earned a Gold Medal in the American Distilling Institute's 10th Annual Judging of Craft Spirits, 2016.

RUM COCKTAILS

RUM AND COKE (CUBA LIBRE)

Fill a short glass with ice. In a shaker, combine

1 1/2 ounces (45 ml) dark rum

Juice of half a lime

Cola to fill

Stir and garnish with a lime wedge.

DAIQUIRI

Fill a short glass with ice. In a shaker, combine

1/2 ounce (45 ml) white rum

1 ounce (30 ml) lime juice

1 tablespoon (15 g) sugar

Ice to fill

Shake and strain into the glass.

PLANTER'S PUNCH

Fill a tall glass with ice. In a shaker, combine

1 1/2 ounces (45 ml) dark rum

1/2 ounce (15 ml) lime juice

1/2 ounce (15 ml) lemon juice

3 ounces (90 ml) orange juice

1 teaspoon (5 g) sugar

Dash grenadine syrup

Ice to fill

Shake and strain into the glass.

Erik and Karin Vonk are turning peanut fields into sugarcane and making rum from it at Richland Distilling Co., Richland, GA.

Cane juice ferments at Ryan and Wood Distillery, Gloucester, MA.

THE BASIS OF RUM

Rum, and its fraternal twin, cane spirit, are made by distilling fermented sugar and water. This sugar comes from the sugarcane and is fermented from cane juice, concentrated cane juice, or molasses. Molasses is the sweet, sticky residue that remains after sugarcane juice is boiled and the crystallized sugar is extracted.

Most rum is made from molasses. Molasses is more than 50 percent sugar, but it also contains significant amounts of minerals and other trace elements, which can contribute to the final flavor. Rums made from cane juice, primarily on Haiti and Martinique, have a naturally smooth palate.

Depending on the recipe, the "wash" (the cane juice or molasses and water) is fermented, using either cultured yeast or airborne wild yeasts, for a period ranging from 24 hours for light rums up to several weeks for heavy, full varieties.

DISTILLATION OF RUM

Rum can be distilled in either pot or column stills. The choice of stills has a profound effect on the final character of the rum.

All rums come out of the still as clear, colorless spirits. Barrel aging and the use of added caramel determine the final color. Because caramel is burnt sugar, it is true that only natural coloring agents are used.

Lighter rums are highly rectified (purified) and are produced in column or continuous stills, then usually charcoal filtered and sometimes aged in old oak casks for a few months to add smoothness. Most light rums have minimal flavors and aromas and are very similar to vodka. Heavier rums are usually distilled in pot stills, similar to those used to produce Cognacs and Scotch whiskeys. Pot stills are less efficient than column stills and some congeners (fusel oils and other flavor elements) are carried over with the alcohol. These heavier rums are used for making golden and dark rums.

Some brands of rum are made by blending pot- and column-distilled rums in a manner similar to that of Armagnac production.

Rusticator Rum by Spirits of Maine Distillery earned a Gold Medal in the American Distilling Institute's 10th Annual Judging of Craft Spirits, 2016.

Maggie's Farm Queen's Share Double Barrel Rum by Allegheny Distilling.

RUM REGIONS

THE CARIBBEAN

The Caribbean is the epicenter of world rum production. Virtually every major island group produces its own distinct rum style.

BARBADOS produces light, sweetish rums from both pot and column stills. Rum distillation began here, and the Mount Gay Distillery, dating from 1663, is probably the oldest operating rum producer in the world.

CUBA produces light-bodied, crisp, clean rums from column stills. It is currently illegal to ship Cuban rums into the United States.

THE DOMINICAN REPUBLIC is notable for its full-bodied, aged rums from column stills.

GUYANA is justly famous for its rich, heavy demerara rums, named for a local river, which are produced from both pot and column stills. Demerara rums can be aged for extended periods (25-year-old varieties are on the market) and are frequently used for blending with lighter rums from other regions. Neighboring Surinam and French Guyana produce similar full-bodied rums.

HAITI follows the French tradition of heavier rums that are double-distilled in pot stills and aged in oak casks for three or more years to produce full-flavored, exceptionally smooth-tasting rums. Haiti also still has an extensive underground moonshine industry that supplies the voodoo religious ritual trade.

JAMAICA is well known for its rich, aromatic rums, most of which are produced in pot stills. Jamaica has official classifications of rum, ranging from light to very full-flavored. Jamaican rums are used extensively for blending.

MARTINIQUE is a French island with the largest number of distilleries in the Eastern Caribbean. Both pot and column stills are used. As on other French islands such as Guadeloupe, both *rhum agricole* (made from sugarcane juice) and *rhum industriel* (made from molasses) are produced. These rums are frequently aged in used French brandy casks for a minimum of three years. *Rhum vieux* (aged rum) is frequently compared to high-quality French brandies.

PUERTO RICO is known primarily for light, very dry rums from column stills. All Puerto Rican rums must, by law, be aged for a minimum of one year.

TRINIDAD produces mainly light rums from column stills and has an extensive export trade.

THE VIRGIN ISLANDS

The Virgin Islands, which are divided between the United States Virgin Islands and the British Virgin Islands, both produce light, mixing rums from column stills. These rums, and those of nearby Grenada, also serve as the base for bay rum, a classic aftershave lotion.

CENTRAL AMERICA

Central America has a variety of primarily medium-bodied rums from column stills that lend themselves well to aging. They have recently begun to gain international recognition.

SOUTH AMERICA

South America produces vast quantities of mostly light rums from column stills, with unaged cane spirit from Brazil, called *cachaça*, being the best-known example. Venezuela bucks this general trend with a number of well-respected barrel-aged golden and dark rums.

NORTH AMERICA

North America has a handful of traditional rum distilleries in the southern United States, producing a range of light- and medium-bodied rums that are generally marketed with Caribbean-themed names. Modern craft distilleries producing rum have skyrocketed from a handful a decade ago to more than 300. Craft producers are generally making a style to rum that is dryer than their Caribbean counterparts and they have sprung up in many locations not usually associated with rum.

Dry Spiced Rum by Cotton & Reed, a distillery bar in Washington, DC, started by two former NASA engineers.

Particularly noteworthy producers including Prichard's Distillery in Kelso, Tennessee; Montanya Distillers in Crested Butte, Colorado; Louisiana Spirits in Lacassine, Louisiana; Malahat Spirits in San Diego, California; Maggie's Farm Rum Distillery in Pittsburgh, Pennsylvania; Privateer Rum Distillery in Ipswich, Massachusetts, and Wicked Dolphin in Cape Coral, Florida.

CANADA

In Canada, the 300-year-old tradition of trading rum for dried codfish continues in the Atlantic maritime provinces of Newfoundland and Nova Scotia, where golden rums from Antigua, Barbados, and Jamaica are imported and aged for five years. The resulting hearty rum is known locally as screech.

EUROPE

Europe is primarily a blender of imported rums. Both the United Kingdom and France import rums from their former colonies in the Caribbean for aging and bottling. Heavy, dark Jamaican rums are imported into Germany and mixed with neutral spirit at a 1 : 19 ratio to produce rum verschnitt. A similar product in Austria is called inlander rum.

The tasting room at Cane Land Distilling Co., Baton Rouge, LA.

Sagatiba Pura Cachaça (Brazil).

Doug Charboneau, left, and his son Jean Luc at the Charboneau Distillery, Natchez, MS.

Ed Haik at Cajun Spirits Distillery, New Orleans, LA.

AUSTRALIA AND OCEANA

Australia produces substantial amounts of white and golden rums in a double-distillation method utilizing both column and pot stills. Rum is the second most popular alcoholic beverage in the country after beer. Light rums are also produced on some of the islands in the South Pacific such as Tahiti and Fiji, and Indian Ocean islands such as Mauritius and Madagascar.

ASIA

In Asia, rums tend to follow regional sugarcane production, with white and golden rums from column stills being produced primarily in the Philippines and Thailand.

WHEN IS RUM NOT RUM? WHEN IT IS CACHAÇA, OF COURSE

Brazil is one of the major sugarcane-growing regions in the world, but there is no local rum, as such, to be found in bars and stores. Instead there is *cachaça*, which Brazilians patriotically insist is a unique local spirit. Less starry-eyed foreign drinkers would classify it as a sugarcane juice spirit similar to *rhum agricole* from French island rum regions. The quality of *cachaça* can vary widely, ranging from inexpensive brands (where the sugarcane spirit is mixed with industrial ethanol in a manner similar to *mixto* tequila or American blended whiskey) to well-aged artisan *cachaças* produced in pot stills and matured in oak barrels.

" ALL TEQUILA IS
MEZCAL, BUT NOT ALL
MEZCAL IS TEQUILLA. "
Tequila marketing mantra

Chapter 8
TEQUILA
AND AGAVE
SPIRITS

The agave plant, a native of Central
America, provides the fermentable
basis for a variety of distilled
spirits, of which tequila is the best
known, but by no means the only
example.

THE EVOLUTION OF TEQUILA

A jimador harvests blue agave for making tequila in Jalisco, Mexico.

In 1656, the village of Tequila (named for the local Ticuilas Indians) was granted a charter by the governor of New Galicia. Tax records of the time show that mezcal was already being produced in the area. This mezcal, made from the local blue agave, established a reputation for having a superior taste, and barrels of the "mezcal wine from Tequila" were soon being shipped to nearby Guadalajara and more distant cities such as the silver-mining boomtowns of San Luis Potosí and Aguascalientes.

The oldest of the still-existing distilleries in Tequila dates back to 1795, when the Spanish crown granted a distiller's license to Jose Cuervo. In 1805, a distillery was established that would ultimately come under the control of the Sauza family. By the mid-1800s, there were dozens of distilleries and millions of agave plants under cultivation around Tequila in what had become the state of Jalisco. Gradually, the locally produced mezcal came to be known as tequila (just as the grape brandy from the Cognac region in France came to be known simply as Cognac).

Mexico achieved independence from Spain in 1821. Until the 1870s, it was a politically unstable country that experienced frequent changes in government, revolutions, and a disastrous war with the United States. Marauding bands of soldiers and guerillas extracted "revolutionary taxes" and "voluntary" contributions in kind from the taverns and distilleries. In 1876, a general named Porfirio Díaz, who was from the mezcal-producing state of Oaxaca (oah-HA-kuh), came to power and ushered in a 35-year period of relative peace and stability known as the *Porfiriato*.

It was during this period that the tequila industry became firmly established. Modest exports of tequila began to the United States and Europe, with Jose Cuervo shipping the first three barrels to El Paso, Texas, in 1873. By 1910, the number of agave distilleries in the state of Jalisco had grown to almost a hundred.

The collapse of the Díaz regime in 1910 led to a decade-long period of revolution that inhibited the tequila industry. The return of peace in the 1920s led to the expansion of tequila production in Jalisco beyond the area around the town of Tequila, with growth being particularly noteworthy in the highlands around the village of Arandas. This period also saw the adoption of modern production techniques from the wine industry, such as cultivated yeast and microbiological sanitary practices.

In the 1930s, the practice of adding non-agave sugars to the aguamiel, or "honey water," was introduced and quickly adopted by many tequila producers. These *mixto* (mixed) tequilas had a less intense taste than 100 percent blue agave tequilas. But this relative blandness also made them more appealing to nonnative consumers, particularly those in the United States.

THE BASIS OF TEQUILA AND MEZCAL

Tequila and mezcal are made by distilling the fermented juice of agave plants in Mexico. The agave is a spiky-leafed member of the lily family (it is not a cactus) and is related to the century plant. By Mexican law, the agave spirit called tequila can be made only from one particular type of agave, the blue agave (*Agave tequilana Weber*), and it can be produced only in specifically designated geographic areas, primarily the state of Jalisco in west-central Mexico. Mezcal is made from the fermented juice of other species of agave. It is produced throughout most of Mexico. Racilla is a mezcal made from non-blue agave in Jalisco.

Both tequila and mezcal are prepared for distillation in similar ways. The agave, also know as *maguey* (pronounced muh-GAY), is cultivated on plantations for eight to ten years, depending on the type of agave. When the plant reaches sexual maturity, it starts to grow a flower stalk. The agave farmer, or *campesino*, cuts off the stalk just as it is starting to grow. This redirects the plant growth into the central stalk, swelling it into a large, bulbous shape that contains a sweet juicy pulp. When the swelling is completed, the *campesino* cuts the plant from its roots and removes the long sword-shaped leaves, using a razor-sharp, pike-like tool called a *coa*. The remaining *piña* ("pineapple"—so-called because the cross-thatched, denuded bulb resembles a giant green-and-white pineapple) weighs anywhere from 25 to 100 pounds.

At the distillery, the *piñas* are cut into quarters. For tequila, they are then slowly baked in steam ovens or autoclaves until all of the starch has been converted to sugars. For mezcal, they are baked in underground ovens heated with wood charcoal (which gives mezcal its distinctive smoky taste). They are then crushed (traditionally with a stone wheel drawn around a circular trough by a mule) and shredded to extract the sweet juice, called *aguamiel* (honey water).

WHAT BING CROSBY AND JIMMY BUFFETT HAVE IN COMMON

Modest amounts of tequila had been exported into U.S. border towns since the late nineteenth century. The first major boost to tequila sales in the United States came in the late 1940s when the Margarita cocktail, a blend of tequila, lime juice, orange liqueur, and ice, was invented. Its origins are uncertain, but Hollywood actors and cocktail parties in California and Mexican resorts seem to be involved in most of the genesis stories. It is known that crooner and actor Bing Crosby was so taken with one particular brand of tequila, Herradura, that he teamed up with fellow actor Phil Harris to import the brand into the United States. The margarita, along with the Tequila Sunrise and the Tequila Sour, have become highly popular in the United States; in fact, it is claimed by many in the liquor industry that the Margarita is the single most popular cocktail in the nation. In the 1970s, when balladeer Jimmy Buffett sang of "wasting away again in Margaritaville," the success of the song enticed millions more Americans to sip from the salt-rimmed Margarita glass.

A bottle of Agua Azul, a blue agave eau de vie.

Barrels set for aging tequila in a warehouse/tasting room.

FERMENTATION: AGAVE OR MIXTO

The fermentation stage determines whether the final product will be 100 percent agave or *mixto*. The highest-quality tequila is made from fermenting and then distilling only agave juice mixed with some water. *Mixto* is made by fermenting and then distilling a mix of agave juice and other sugars, usually cane sugar with water. *Mixtos* made and bottled in Mexico can contain up to 40 percent alcohol made from other sugars. *Mixtos* that have been shipped in bulk to other countries (primarily the United States) for bottling may have the agave content further reduced to 51 percent by the foreign bottler. By Mexican law, all 100 percent agave or aged tequilas must be bottled in Mexico. If a tequila is 100 percent agave, it will always say so on the bottle label. If it doesn't say 100 percent, it is a *mixto*, although that term is seldom used on bottle labels.

DISTILLATION AND AGING OF TEQUILA AND MEZCAL

Traditionally, tequila and mezcal have been distilled in pot stills at 110° proof (55 percent ABV). The resulting spirit is clear but contains a significant amount of congeners and other flavor elements. Some light-colored tequilas are now being rectified (redistilled) in column stills to produce a cleaner, blander spirit.

Color in tequila and mezcal comes mostly from the addition of caramel, although barrel aging is a factor in some high-quality brands. Additionally, some distillers add small amounts of natural flavorings such as sherry, prune concentrate, and coconut to manipulate the product's flavor profile. These added flavors do not stand out, by themselves, but instead serve to smooth out the often hard-edged palate of agave spirit.

MEZCAL AND THE WORM

The rules and regulations that govern the production and packaging of tequila do not apply to agave spirits produced outside of the designated areas in Mexico. Some mezcal distilleries are very primitive and very small. The best known mezcals come from the southern state of Oaxaca, although they are produced in a number of other states. Eight varieties of agave are approved for mezcal production, but the chief variety used is the espadin agave (*Agave angustifolia Haw*).

The famous worm found in some bottles of mezcal (*"con gusano"*) is the larva of one of two moths that live on the agave plant. The reason for adding the worm to the bottle of mezcal is obscure. But one story, which at least has the appeal of logic to back it up, is that the worm serves as proof of high proof: The worm remains intact in the bottle if the percentage of alcohol in the spirit is high enough to preserve the pickled worm. Consuming the worm, which can be done without harm, has served as a rite of passage for generations of fraternity boys. Top-quality mezcals do not include a worm in the bottle.

Cinco de Noviembre Mezcal by Kimo
Sabe Mezcal.

From the 1930s through the 1980s,
the bulk of the tequila being produced
was of the blended *mixto* variety. The
original 100 percent agave tequilas
were reduced to a minor specialty
product in the market. In the late
1980s, the rising success of single-
malt Scotch and expensive Cognacs
in the international marketplace
did not go unnoticed among tequila
producers. New brands of 100 percent
blue agave tequilas were introduced,
and sales began a steady growth curve
that continues to this day.

Brendan Moylan holds up a couple of bottles of
JB Wagoner's 100 percent Blue Agave Spirits in
front of his well-stocked bar.

THE SPIRIT OF MEXICO IS MORE THAN JUST AGAVE

In the northern Mexican states of Chihuahua, Coahulia, and Durango, a local evergreen shrub called the dasylirion is used to produce sotol, a crisp spirit with dry metallic notes. *Aguardiente* (roughly translated as "firewater") is an unaged, frequently raw spirit that is distilled from pretty much whatever fermentable organic base product is available. Drink at your own risk.

NON-MEXICAN AGAVE SPIRITS

Federal excise tax records indicate that tequila-like agave spirits were produced in the 1930s in the southwestern United States. Recently, more than a dozen modern craft distillers have begun to experiment with their own agave spirits, such as El Ladron Agave Spirit by Venus Spirits in Santa Cruz, California; Agua Azul by St. George Spirits in Alameda, California; and El Keyote by Cannon Beach Distillery in Cannon Beach, Oregon; The Wise King Anejo Agave Spirit by State 38 Distilling, Golden Colorado, and Frontera Norte Agave by Flying Dutchman Spirits in Eden Prarie, Minnesota.

CLASSIFICATIONS OF TEQUILA

Beyond the two basic designations of tequila—agave and *mixto*—there are four categories:

STYLE	DEFINITION	HOWEVER...
Silver or Blanco	Clear, with little (no more than 60 days in stainless steel tanks) or no aging. They can be either 100 percent agave or *mixto*. Silver tequilas are used primarily for mixing and blend particularly well into fruit-based drinks.	Once you have confirmed that it is 100 percent blue agave, a fancy bottle and a higher price do not necessarily mean that it is a better spirit.
Gold	Unaged silver tequila that has been colored and flavored with caramel. It is usually a *mixto*.	A product category produced primarily for silly gringos. Serious tequila drinkers go for reposados.
Reposado/Rested	"Rested" tequila is aged in wooden tanks or casks for a legal minimum period of at least two months, with the better-quality brands spending three to nine months in wood. It can be either 100 percent agave or *mixto*.	Reposado tequilas are the best-selling tequilas in Mexico.
Añejo/Aged	"Old" tequila is aged in wooden barrels (usually old bourbon barrels) for a minimum of 12 months. The best-quality anejos are aged for 18 months to three years for *mixtos*, and up to four years for 100 percent agaves.	Aging tequila for more than four years is a matter of controversy. Most tequila producers oppose doing so because they feel that "excessive" oak aging will overwhelm the distinctive earthy and vegetal agave flavor notes.

El Ladron Agave Spirit by Venus Spirits, Santa Cruz, CA.

AS THE WORM TURNS

The upgrading and upscaling of tequila has, in turn, inspired mezcal producers to undertake similar measures. In the past few years, an increasing number of high-end mezcals, including some intriguing "single village" bottlings, have been introduced to the market. Mezcal now seems to be coming into its own as a distinctive, noteworthy spirit.

TEQUILA COCKTAILS

CLASSIC MARGARITA

Take a short glass. Wet the rim with lime juice. Put the glass upside down in coarse salt, so that the salt clings to the rim. In a cocktail shaker, combine:

1 1/2 ounces (45 ml) silver tequila

3/4 ounce (23 ml) triple sec

3/4 ounce (23 ml) lime juice

Ice to fill

Shake and strain into the salt-rimmed glass and garnish with a lime slice.

FROZEN FRUIT MARGARITA

Take a short glass. Wet the rim with lime juice and put the glass upside down in coarse salt, so salt clings to the rim (this step is optional). Combine the ingredients for the Classic Margarita in a blender with very ripe fruit (6 to 7 ounces [170 to 200 g] fresh or 4 ounces [115 g] frozen). Add 3/4 cup ice. Blend until smooth and pour into the glass.

TEQUILA SUNRISE

Fill a tall glass with ice. Add:

1 1/2 ounces (45 ml) silver tequila

Orange juice almost to full

Slowly pour 1/2 ounce (15 ml) grenadine syrup over the top. (As it trickles down, it creates the "sunrise" effect.)

El Keyote Agave Spirit from Cannon Beach Distilley, Cannon Beach, OR.

The Wise King Anejo Agave Spirit by State 38 Distilling, Golden Colorado.

Chapter 9
INFUSED SPIRITS: LIQUEURS, SCHNAPPS, ANISE, AND BITTERS

—

LIQUORS can refer generically to distilled spirits, but they can also be specifically flavored spirits. Add a sweetener and they become liqueurs. Add certain herbs and you now have bitters. At the end of the day, if something can be fermented and then distilled, people will drink it.

Liqueurs, schnapps, anise, amari, and bitters are terms that cover a wide variety of types of spirits. What they all share in common is that they are infused, or flavored, spirits.

LIQUEURS

Also known as cordials, liqueurs are sweet, flavor-infused spirits that are categorized according to the flavoring agent (fruits, nuts, herbal and spice blends, creams, and such). The word liqueur comes from the Latin *liquifacere* ("to dissolve") and refers to the dissolving of flavorings in the spirits. Artificial flavorings are strictly regulated in most countries and where allowed they must be prominently labeled as such.

Top-quality liqueurs are produced by distillation of either the fermented flavor materials or the spirit in which they have been infused. Many liqueurs use finished spirits such as Cognac, rum, or whiskey as their base. Others macerate fruit or other flavorings in a neutral spirit. Crèmes (crème de menthe, crème de cacao, etc.) are liqueurs with a primary flavor, while cream liqueurs combine dairy cream and alcohol in a homogenized, shelf-stable blend.

Liqueurs are not usually aged for any great length of time, but they may undergo resting stages during their production to allow the various flavors to "marry" into a harmonious blend. Some Italian amari are rested in barrels for several years as the complex botanical mixtures combine into deep flavors.

Townshend's Distillery in Portland, OR, produces a line of spirits, including herbal liqueurs, from excess alcohol extracted from their Brew Dr. Kombucha.

Freshly filled bottles of Raspberry Liqueur await boxing and shipping at the Sidetrack Distillery in Kent, WA.

Unripened black walnuts are infused in high-proof alcohol in the process of making Nocino, an Italian-style bitter liqueur at Sidetrack Distillery in Kent, WA.

BLENDED FAMILIES

All liqueurs are blends, even those with a primary flavor. A touch of vanilla is added to crème de cacao to emphasize the chocolate. Citrus flavor notes sharpen the presentation of anise. Herbal liqueurs may contain dozens of different flavor elements that a master blender manipulates to achieve the desired flavor profile.

Maple Liqueur by Salish Sea Organic Liqueurs earned a Gold Medal in the American Distilling Intitute's 2018 International Judging of Craft Spirits.

Raspberry Liqueur by Skip Rock Distillers earned a Gold Medal in the American Distilling Institute's 2018 International Judging of Craft Spirits.

Helgolander German style Herbal Liqueur by the Dampfwerk Distillery Co. earned a Gold Medal in the American Distilling Institute's 2018 International Judging of Craft Spirits.

Black Walnut Liqueur by Wood Hat Spirits earned a Gold Medal in the American Distilling Intitute's 2018 International Judging of Craft Spirits.

A. van Wees De Ooievaar fruit liqueur from the Netherlands.

Rosolis Ziolowy Gorzki is a rose-flavored stomach bitters from the Lancut Distillery in Poland.

Liqueurs can be hard to classify, but regardless of flavor they can be broadly divided into two categories. Generics are liqueurs of a particular type (crème de cacao or curaçao, for example) that can be made by any producer. Proprietaries are liqueurs with trademarked names that are made according to a specific formula. Examples of such liqueurs include Kahlúa, Grand Marnier, and Southern Comfort.

SCHNAPPS

Schnapps is a general term used for an assortment of white and flavored spirits that have originated in northern countries or regions, such as Germany or Scandinavia. Schnapps can be made from grain, potatoes, or molasses and can be flavored with virtually anything (watermelon and root beer schnapps from the United States being proof of that). The dividing line between schnapps and flavored vodka is vague and is more cultural than stylistic.

Label for Johnny Ziegler Black Forest Style Apple Aux Pommel Schnapps Eau de Vie by Winegarden Estate in New Brunswick, Canada.

Label for Blackberry Liqueur by Clear Creek Distillery.

ANISE-FLAVORED SPIRITS

These spirits can vary widely in style, depending on the country of origin. They can be dry or very sweet, low or high proof, distilled from fermented aniseed or macerated in neutral spirit.

In France, anis (as produced by Pernod) is produced by distilling anise and a variety of other botanicals together. Pastis is macerated, rather than distilled, and contains fewer botanicals than anis. In Italy, sambuca is distilled from anise and botanicals, but it is then heavily sweetened to make it a liqueur. Oil of fennel (also known as green anise) is frequently added to boost the aroma of the spirit. Greece has a drier, grappa-like liqueur called ouzo, which is stylistically close to pastis.

Absent Minded is an organic absinthe by Wigle Whiskey, in Pittsburgh, PA.

Wildcard Absinthe by Oregon Spirit Distillers, earned a Double-Gold Medal, Best of Category and Best of Class at the American Distilling Institute's 9th Annual Judging of Craft American Spirits.

Black Note Amaro by Turin Vermouth, Italy.

Absinthe Verte by St. George Spirits.

Absinthe Verte by Leopold Bros.

Kevin Herson makes three different styles of absinthe at Doc Herson's Natural Spirits, Brooklyn, NY.

ABSINTHE MAKES THE HEART GROW FONDER

Modern pastis is the genteel descendent of its much more raffish nineteenth-century ancestor absinthe, a high-(sometimes very high) proof anise liquor (technically not a liqueur because no sugar is added) that included extract of wormwood in its list of botanicals. Wormwood contains the chemical compound thujone, whose alleged psychedelic effects made absinthe very popular among the bohemian counterculture artists and intellectuals of France and Europe (Vincent van Gogh and Oscar Wilde were devotees of what was termed the Green Fairy). Conversely, social conservatives and prohibitionists campaigned against it as the crack cocaine of its day and eventually got it outlawed in most European countries and the United States. Modern scientific analysis has found thujone's psychedelic potency to be, at best, greatly exaggerated and many distillers claim most of the thujone in absinthe comes from anise and not wormwood.

Forbidden fruit is always appealing, and starting in the 1990s, absinthe, which continued to be commercially produced in Eastern Europe, slowly started to return to the general marketplace, initially in "thujone-free" versions from France and Switzerland. When absinthe was again legalized in the U.S,, St. George Spirits in Alameda, California, jumped in to be the first brand approved and many others have followed suit. One thing that has not changed about absinthe is its high alcohol content.

BITTERS AND AMARI

The modern-day descendants of medieval medical potions, bitters are marketed as having at least some vaguely therapeutic value (stomach settlers, hangover cures, and so on). They tend to be flavored with herbs, roots, and botanicals and contain lower quantities of fruit and sugar than liqueurs.

The Farmaceutica di Santa Maria Novella, in Florence, Italy, founded in 1612, produces *amari* (plural of *amaro*: Italian bitter liqueurs) from recipes that date back to the 17th century. Some European aperitifs and digestifs have been lifted from obscurity in recent years from active marketing campaigns. Fernet Branca, another Italian amaro from Milan has gained popularity with American bartenders for an end-of-the-night shot. Jägermeister was a German old man's drink, most often served at room temperature in small quantities to warm a body on cold, damp winter days, until a clever marketing campaign made it popular as a shooter served colder than an ice cube to American college students.

These digestifs—ranging from the dry Unicum from Hungary to the sweet Becherovka from the Czech Republic—are produced in almost every country in Europe, while new American producers are getting into the game.

Italian immigrant Francesco Amodeo founded Don Ciccio & Figli with recipes his family produced and sold on the Amalfi Coast from 1883 until an earthquake destroyed the production facility in 1980. His plant in Washington, DC, produces limoncello and a variety of amari. Another DC-based amaro producer, Founding Spirits, makes amaro at a nanodistillery inside the Founding Farmers restaurant. Fernet Michaud, by Liquid Riot in Portland, Maine, is another fine example of a modern craft distillery producing their own version of a European classic. Underground Herbal Spirit, produced by Ogden's Own in Utah, is also a noteworthy example of the style.

As bartenders scoured through 19th-century recipes looking for classic cocktails to revive, spirits producers have scrambled to resurrect long-lost spirits, often found in 19th-century pharmacy notebooks. St. Germain elderflower liqueur rocketed to popularity when it caught the fancy of bartenders. The Woodinville, Washington, distillery broVo Spirits created a line of more than a dozen amari by working with individual bartenders to create their dream amaro.

Although there are specialty liqueur producers, most brands are produced by general distillers as part of an extended product line. Among the new generation of craft distillers, some of the standout liqueur producers include Leopold Brothers Distillery of Denver, Colorado, with their distinctive whiskey-based fruit liqueurs (the Rocky Mountain Blackberry is particularly noteworthy); Flag Hill Winery and Distillery in Lee, New Hampshire, with their delicately tinged Sugar Maple Liqueur; and Sidetrack Distillery, in Kent, Washington, who produce a variety of eaux de vie and liqueurs using produce from the farm adjacent to the distillery.

ROCKY MOUNTAIN PEACH
FLAVORED WHISKEY

LEOPOLD BROS.

The finest Colorado Peaches from the Western Slopes of the Rockies are harvested beginning in late July, juiced, and blended with our small batch whiskey. We then place the spirit into used bourbon barrels for further maturation, allowing the intense peach flavors to marry with the whiskey. The final step is a rough filtration that removes any leftover fruit pulp without stripping away any of the flavors. This is the very essence of a Rocky Mountain Peach, coupled with an American Small Batch Whiskey, painstakingly preserved in a hand-numbered bottle.

30% ALC. BY VOL.   BATCH NO. 1104   750 ML

Rocky Mountain Peach Flavored Whiskey by Leopold Bros.

Todd Leopold is highly regarded among his fellow distillers for holding high standards and renovating old techniques, including floor malting and recreating a 19th-century style of chambered still. Leopold Bros. fruit-flavored whiskeys are among his highly acclaimed spirits.

Francesco Amodeo, left, and Jonathan Fasano at Don Ciccio & Figli, a rectifier making amari and other Italian liqueurs from old family recipes, in Washington, DC.

Chapter 10
DISTILLING RESOURCES

—

BEFORE you are going to walk the walk, you first need to learn the talk.

The Distiller's Library is a bibliography of English-language books on distilling and the various types of spirits. If you haven't already found what you want in this book, well, here are a whole lot of alternative sources.

The Distiller's Glossary will help you sort out the industry jargon that is sprinkled throughout the text of this book. Learning the meaning of the term slobber box, alone, is worth the price of admission.

And finally, the International Directory of Distilleries is a link to the most comprehensive worldwide listing of operating whiskey and craft distilleries as maintained by the American Distilling Institute. So many tots of whiskey to sample, so little time.

THE DISTILLER'S LIBRARY

WHEN it comes to learning about what they make, craft brewers have it relatively easy. Since Michael Jackson's first book on beer came out in the early 1980s, there has been a steady flood of consumer and professional books on beer and brewing arriving on the market. Not so for spirits until fairly recently. The selection is better than it used to be. Here is a bibliographic summary of what is available.

NOTE: Not all of these books are currently in print, but as of this book's publication, they were all available through Amazon.com or Alibrus.com. The review comments are solely the opinions of the editor, Alan Dikty.

DISTILLED SPIRITS, GENERAL

Blue, Anthony Dias.

THE COMPLETE BOOK OF SPIRITS.

New York: HarperCollins Publishers, 2004.

Wide-ranging review of all major categories of spirits by a well-known beverage and lifestyle writer, with tasting notes and cocktail recipes. Its usefulness is marred by truly awful copyediting.

Dikty, Alan S.

BUYING GUIDE TO SPIRITS.

New York: Sterling Publishing, 1999.

Concise but detailed chapters on all spirits categories, with thousands of tasting notes. Used as a training manual for the sales force of the largest liquor wholesaler in the United States. Written, with a certain dry wit, by the editor of this book.

Henriques, E. Frank.

THE SIGNET ENCYCLOPEDIA OF WHISKEY, BRANDY & ALL OTHER SPIRITS.

New York: Signet, New American Library, 1979.

CliffsNotes for bar management: quick but informative reference descriptions and explanations for thousands of spirit types, brands and cocktails. Out of print, but worth searching out.

Lembeck, Harriet.

GROSSMAN'S GUIDE TO WINES, BEERS, AND SPIRITS.

New York: Charles Scribner's Sons, 1983.

The grand old reference guide to alcoholic beverages: the spirits section is still a good introduction to all the major and many, many of the minor categories and brands.

A bartender eyes her pour carefully while serving three Blood on Sand cocktails.

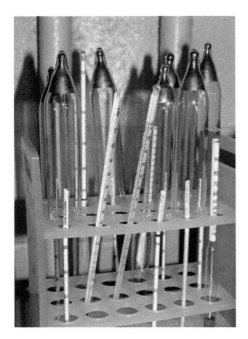

Hydrometers for measuring alcohol content of distillates.

Owens, Bill, ed.

WORLD GUIDE TO WHISKEY DISTILLERIES.

White Mule Press, 2009. www.distilling.com

A complete listing of whiskey distilleries.

Price, Pamela Vandyke.

A DIRECTORY OF WINES AND SPIRITS.

London: Peerage Books, 1986.

More wine than spirits oriented, but any reference book that tells the truth about Southern Comfort (it contains no bourbon) is worthwhile.

DISTILLED SPIRITS, HISTORY

Barr, Andrew.

DRINK: A SOCIAL HISTORY OF AMERICA.

New York: Carroll & Graf Publishers, 1999. Breezy but well-researched history of drinking in the United States, combined with droll put-downs of prohibitionists past and especially present.

Fleming, Alice.

ALCOHOL: THE DELIGHTFUL POISON.

New York: Laurel-Leaf Library, Dell Publishing, 1975.

Short history of world and American spirits, followed by an extended essay on the physical effects (positive and negative) of alcohol.

Forbes, R. J.

SHORT HISTORY OF THE ART OF DISTILLATION.

Leiden: E. J. Brill, 1948.

White Mule Press reprinting of a Dutch history of distillation from Ptolemaic Egypt to the advent of column distillation in the mid-19th century. Many, many illustrations.

Gately, Ian.

DRINK: A CULTURAL HISTORY OF ALCOHOL.

New York: Gotham Books, 2009.

Excellent world history of the development of the drinking of alcohol and how its production, including distilling, has influenced various cultures.

Ganong, Niki.

THE FIELD GUIDE TO DRINKING IN AMERICA: A TRAVELER'S HANDBOOK TO STATE LIQUOR LAWS.

Portland, OR: Overcup Press, 2015.

Planning on selling your craft spirits across state lines? This breezy, graphic-heavy consumer guide contains a surprising amount of useful information on the local quirks of selling alcohol in all 50 states.

Heron, Craig.

BOOZE: A DISTILLED HISTORY.

Toronto: Between the Lines, 2003.

A history of liquor in Canada, written from a feminist, politically correct (!) point of view. Lots of informative history, eh?

Lender, Mark Edward, and James Kirby Martin.

DRINKING IN AMERICA: A HISTORY.

New York: The Free Press, 1982.

Conventional but well-written survey of liquor drinking in the United States, from Colonial times to the present. Heavily illustrated.

Logsdon, Gene.

GOOD SPIRITS.

White River Junction, VT: Chelsea Green, 1999.

A social history of distillation in the United States, and a call for home distillation. The author is a bit of a crank, but writes well.

Moss, Robert F.

SOUTHERN SPIRITS: FOUR HUNDRED YEARS OF DRINKING IN THE AMERICAN SOUTH, WITH RECIPES.

Berkeley: Ten Speed Press, 2016.

A social history of drinking spirits in the American South from Colonial times through to the present bourbon whiskey boom, with many cocktail recipes.

Rorabaugh, W. J.

THE ALCOHOL REPUBLIC: AN AMERICAN TRADITION.

New York: Oxford University Press, 1979.

In the United States, 1790 to 1830 was the high tide of spirits consumption. Everyone drank, there were no excise taxes, all distilleries were small and local and best of all, there was no organized temperance movement. Ah, the good old days!

Spivak, Mark.

ICONIC SPIRITS: AN INTOXICATED HISTORY.

Guilford, CT: Lyons Press, 2012.

A breezy history of how twelve spirits, from moonshine to tequila, influenced world history, written by an NPR presenter for the NPR crowd — you know who you are.

Waxman, Max.

CHASING THE WHITE DOG.

Simon & Schuster, 2009.

Tracing the historical roots of moonshine through the backwoods of the United States.

Wilson, Jason.

BOOZEHOUND: ON THE TRAIL OF THE RARE, THE OBSCURE, AND THE OVERRATED IN SPIRITS.

Berkeley: Ten Speed Press, 2010.

A veteran newspaper beverage columnist surveys the current spirits market scene, dishes some cocktail recipes, and pricks more than a few marketing bubbles.

DISTILLED SPIRITS, MEDICINAL EFFECTS

Center for Science in the Public Interest.

CHEMICAL ADDITIVES IN BOOZE.

Washington, DC: CSPI Books, 1982.

The CSPI is a notorious collection of public scolds, and no friend to distilled spirits. But their chemical analysis of assorted brands of wines, spirits, and beers makes interesting reading. Hint: Stay away from any liqueur with the word crème in the brand name.

Chafetz, Morris E.

LIQUOR: THE SERVANT OF MAN.

Boston: Little Brown, 1965.

Don't let drunken fools screw it up for the rest of us, explained in 223 pages.

Ford, Gene.

THE BENEFITS OF MODERATE DRINKING: ALCOHOL, HEALTH, & SOCIETY.

San Francisco: Wine Appreciation Guild, 1988.

Listen to your doctor. Wine (and spirits) in moderation are good for you.

DISTILLED SPIRITS, PHILOSOPHY

Allhoff, Fritz, ed.

WHISKEY AND PHILOSOPHY.

John Wiley & Sons, 2009.

Philosophy of consuming and discussion of whiskey.

Amis, Kingsley.

ON DRINK.

New York: Harcourt Brace Jovanovich, 1972.

One of Britain's great postwar novelists discusses the purpose of drinking in a series of essays where the wit is as dry as his recipe for a martini.

DeVoto, Bernard.

THE HOUR.

Boston: Houghton Mifflin, 1951.

One of the United States's great literary critics of the twentieth century explains the importance of good whiskey in a civil society, along with the importance of a properly made martini in "the violet twilight of each day—the cocktail hour."

Edmunds, Lowell.

THE SILVER BULLET.

Westport, CT: Greenwood Press, 1981.

The martini as a mirror of America's soul. Seven messages from the cocktail shaker.

DISTILLED SPIRITS, PRODUCTION

Hundreds of bottles of spirits line the walls in the ultimate well-stocked bar.

Barleycorn, Michael.

MOONSHINER'S MANUAL.

Hayward, CA: White Mule Press, 2009. www.distilling.com.

Home distillation for beginners.

Byrn, M. Lafayette.

THE COMPLETE PRACTICAL DISTILLER.

Chagrin Falls, OH: Raudins Publishing, 2002. www.raudins.com

Reprinting of 1875 distillery operations manual that contains a lot of still-useful information for a small-scale pot distiller.

Hall, Harrison.

THE DISTILLER.

San Francisco: Knowledge Arts Media, 2013.

White Mule Press 2015 reprint of an 1818 professional distiller's manual. Includes a chapter on "The Imitation of Foreign Spirits."

Hoefling, Brian D.

DISTILLED KNOWLEDGE: THE SCIENCE BEHIND DRINKING'S GREATEST MYTHS, LEGENDS, AND UNANSWERED QUESTIONS.

New York: Abbeville Press, 2016.

What goes into a bottle of alcohol, and what it does to your body and that of the zebra finch.

M'Harry, Samuel.

PRACTICAL DISTILLER.

Chagrin Falls, OH: Raudins Publishing, 2001.

Reprinting of 1809 (!) American distilling manual. Learn about distilling techniques from the era of the birth of bourbon. Fascinating reading. Order at www.raudins.com.

Goldsmith, David J.

A PRACTICAL HANDBOOK ON THE DISTILLATION OF ALCOHOL FROM FARM PRODUCTS.

Amsterdam: Fredonia Books, 2001.

Reprint of 1922 distilling manual first published during national Prohibition. Just remember, folks: don't drink it, because that would be illegal, wink, wink. Order at www.fredoniabooks.com.

Murtaugh, Dr. John E.

THE ALCOHOL TEXTBOOK.

Nottingham, UK: Nottingham University Press, 2003.

Commercial-scale ethanol and beverage alcohol production techniques and reference charts. Not for light reading.

Nixon, Mike, and Mike McGaw.

THE COMPLEAT DISTILLER.

Auckland, NZ: Amphora Society, 2001. Advanced home distilling from New Zealand. Lots of practical information for newbies.

Owens, Bill.

CRAFT WHISKEY DISTILLING.

Hayward, CA: White Mule Press, 2009.

www.distilling.com. Compact summary of the small-scale distilling process. Heavily illustrated.

Rogers, Adam.

PROOF: THE SCIENCE OF BOOZE.

Houghton Mifflin Harcourt, 2014.

The production processing and effects of beverage alcohol explained. Geeky, but in a good way.

Rowley, Matthew.

MOONSHINE.

Lark Books, 2006.

How to build a still at home.

Russell, Inge, ed.

WHISKEY TECHNOLOGY.

Academic Press, 2003.

Handbook of alcoholic beverages.

Smiley, Ian.

MAKING PURE CORN WHISKEY: A PROFESSIONAL GUIDE FOR AMATEUR AND MICRO DISTILLERS.

Amphora Society, 2003.
www.home-distilling.com.

A crash course in small-scale distilling from New Zealand, the homeland of modern moonshining.

Stone, John.

MAKING GIN & VODKA.

Vancouver, BC: John Stone, 1997.
www.gin-vodka.com

Advanced home-distilling techniques for white spirits.

BRANDY AND EAU DE VIE

Behrendt, Axel, and Bibiana Behrendt.

COGNAC.

New York: Abbeville Press, 1997.

Detailed tasting notes and histories for more than a hundred producers.

Behrendt, Axel, and Bibiana Behrendt.

GRAPPA: A GUIDE TO THE BEST.

New York: Abbeville Press, 2000.

Extensively researched guide to Italian pomace brandy. Detailed tasting notes and producer histories.

Boudin, Ove.

GRAPPA: ITALY BOTTLED.

Partille: PianoForte Publishing, 2007.

Coffee-table picture book crossed with a surprisingly detailed explanation of how grappa is produced in Italy and who does it.

Brown, Gordon.

HANDBOOK OF FINE BRANDIES.

New York: Macmillan, 1990.

British-oriented guide to the brandies of the world. Odd bar chart product ratings, but still a good general overview of the subject.

Calabrese, Salvatore.

COGNAC: A LIQUID HISTORY.

London: Cassel, 2001.

Big type, lots of pretty pictures, but still a useful reference work, with intelligent tasting notes.

A Ping-Pong table at St. George's Spirits keeps the hardest-working distillers entertained and on their toes in the distillery.

Germain-Robin, Hubert.

TRADITIONAL DISTILLATION: ART AND PASSION.

Hayward: White Mule Press, 2012.

A pioneer California brandy distiller, with family roots in Cognac, muses on brandy distillation and production techniques.

Germain-Robin, Hubert.

THE MATURATION OF DISTILLED SPIRITS: VISION AND PATIENCE.

Hayward: White Mule Press, 2016.

A sixth-generation native of Cognac reveals cellar masters' techniques for nurturing flavor creation in the barrel.

Hannum, Hurst, and Robert S. Blumberg.

BRANDIES AND LIQUEURS OF THE WORLD.

Garden City, NJ: Doubleday, 1976.

Well-written and still useful overview of the brandies of the world.

Herbert, Malcolm.

CALIFORNIA BRANDY CUISINE.

San Francisco: Wine Appreciation Guild, 1984.

Primarily a cooking and mixed, drink recipe book, it also contains historical notes on the California brandy industry prior to the arrival of modern craft distillers.

Mattsson, Henrik.

CALVADOS: THE WORLD'S PREMIER APPLE BRANDY.

Flavourrider AB, 2004.

A Swedish writer's introduction to the apple brandies of Normandy, France. Both a brandy and travel guide, and good at both.

Neal, Charles.

ARMAGNAC: THE DEFINITIVE GUIDE TO FRANCE'S PREMIER BRANDY.

San Francisco: Flame Grape Press, 1998.

Exhaustive guide to every commercial distillery in Armagnac, most of which are tiny farm distilleries. The author loves his topic, hates inferior production techniques, and lets you know exactly what he thinks.

Nicholas, Faith.

COGNAC.

London: Mitchell Beazley, 2005.

Typical flashy-looking Mitchell Beazley beverage book. Quick history, lots of tasting notes on pricey XOs.

Page, C. E.

ARMAGNAC: THE SPIRIT OF GASCONY.

London: Bloomsbury, 1990.

Standard, British-centered guide to Armagnac. Tour and tasting notes.

Ray, Cyril.

COGNAC.

New York: Stein & Day, 1973.

Well-known British wine writer presents a droll history of France's best known brandy.

GIN

Coates, Geraldine.

DISCOVERING GIN.

London: New Lifestyle Publishing, 1996.

Flashy graphics and history lite text on the social history of gin.

Dillon, Patrick.

GIN: THE MUCH-LAMENTED DEATH OF MADAM GENEVA.

Boston: Justin, Charles, 2003.

The story of the eighteenth-century gin craze in England is even stranger than you can imagine.

Emmons, Bob.

THE BOOK OF GINS & VODKAS.

Chicago: Open Court, 2000.

Quick but comprehensive introduction to the two primary white spirits.

Smith, David T.

FORGOTTEN SPIRITS & LOST LIQUEURS.

Hayward: White Mule Press, 2015.

Non–London Dry Gin varieties and so-old-they're-new-again types of bitters described and explained, plus lots of cocktail recipes to show what you can do with them.

Watney, John.

MOTHER'S RUIN: THE STORY OF GIN.

London: Peter Owen, 1976.

The social history of gin in England. Sloe gin explained!

LIQUEUR AND BITTERS

Conrad, Barnaby.

ABSINTHE: HISTORY IN A BOTTLE.

San Francisco: Chronicle Books, 1988.

The crack cocaine of its time, but in truth, much maligned. A social history of the "Green Fairy."

Parsons, Brad Thomas.

BITTERS: A SPIRITED HISTORY OF A CLASSIC CURE-ALL.

Berkeley: Ten Speed Press, 2011.

A crash course in bitters, what they are, who makes them and how to use them.

Walton, Stuart.

THE NEW GUIDE TO SPIRITS AND LIQUEURS.

London: Lorenz Books, 2000.

Well-organized reference guide to liqueurs and how to mix them.

White, Francesca. Cheers!

A SPIRITED GUIDE TO LIQUORS AND LIQUEURS.

London: Paddington Press, 1977.

Capsule explanations of many liqueurs, well known and obscure.

RUM

Arkell, Julie.

CLASSIC RUM.

London: Prion Books, 1999.

Quick-moving survey of rums of the world, with an emphasis on the Caribbean.

Ayala, Luis.

THE RUM EXPERIENCE.

Round Rock, TX: Rum Runner Press, 2001.

Enthusiastic guide to the rums of the Americas. Highly opinionated.

Barty-King, Hugh, and Anton Massel.

RUM: YESTERDAY AND TODAY.

London: Heinemann, 1983.

Serious history of rum in all of its major markets.

Broom, Dave.

RUM.

London: Mitchell Beazley, 2003.

More specifically, rums of the Caribbean for Brit drinkers. Lots of pretty pictures.

Coulombe, Charles A.

RUM: THE EPIC STORY OF THE DRINK THAT CONQUERED THE WORLD.

New York: Citadel Press, 2004.

The political history of rum from a Catholic perspective. (Really!)

Gelabert, Blanche.

THE SPIRIT OF PUERTO RICAN RUM.

San Juan: Discovery Press, 1992.

Cooking and mixing drinks with Puerto Rican rum.

A bottle of Northern Comfort Massachusetts Liqueur sits on the counter at Nashoba Distillery.

The George Washington Distillery.

Hamilton, Edward.

THE COMPLETE GUIDE TO RUM.

Chicago: Triumph Press, 1996.

A yacht-cruising tour of the rums of the Caribbean. A great read.

Hamilton, Edward.

RUMS OF THE EASTERN CARIBBEAN.

Culebra, PR: Tafia Publishing, 1997.

The Minister of Rum recycles *The Complete Guide to Rum.*

Pack, Capt. James

NELSON'S BLOOD: THE STORY OF NAVAL RUM.

Annapolis: Naval Institute Press, 1983.

Rum as a tool of social control in the Royal Navy. So, how much is a tot of rum?

Plotkin, Robert.

CARIBE RUM: THE ORIGINAL GUIDE TO CARIBBEAN RUM AND DRINKS.

Tucson: Bar Media, 2001.

Many, many mixed drink recipes, uniformly enthusiastic product reviews, and a very, very annoying page layout featuring a winged heart (don't ask).

Smiley, Ian; Watson, Eric and Michael Delevante.

THE DISTILLER'S GUIDE TO RUM.

Hayward: White Mule Press, 2013.

A brief history of rum, followed by a detailed explanation of the ingredients and various production techniques used in the distillation of rum. A good, detailed introduction to rum production for entry-level distillers and detail-obsessed rum enthusiasts.

TEQUILA

Emmons, Bob.

THE BOOK OF TEQUILA: A COMPLETE GUIDE.

Chicago: Open Court, 1997.

Truth in advertising. Excellent introduction to the history and production of tequila. Brand listings are now somewhat dated, but still very useful.

Martinez Limon, Enrique.

TEQUILA: THE SPIRIT OF MEXICO.

New York: Abbeville Press, 2000. Extensively illustrated consumer guide to the production and brands of tequila.

Sanchez, Alberto Ruy, and Margarita de Orellana.

TEQUILA: A TRADITIONAL ART OF MEXICO.

Washington: Smithsonian Books, 2004.

Breezy, lightweight guide to current brands of tequila. Lots of drink recipes.

Valenzuela-Zapata, Ana G., and Gary Paul Nabhan.

TEQUILA! A NATURAL AND CULTURAL HISTORY.

Tucson: The University of Arizona Press, 2003.

Tequila as seen through the eyes of plant biologists.

VODKA

Begg, Desmond.

THE VODKA COMPANION.

Philadelphia: Running Press, 1998.

Quick history of vodka with extensive tasting notes.

Delos, Gilbert.

VODKAS OF THE WORLD.

Edison, NJ: Wellfleet Press, 1998.

Excellent survey of vodkas and aquavit.

Wisniewski, Ian.

VODKA: DISCOVERING, EXPLORING, ENJOYING.

London: Ryland Peters & Small, 2003.

A stylish magazine article on vodka turned into a very short book.

WHISKEY, GENERAL

Gabanyi, Stefan.

WHISK(E)Y.

New York: Abbeville Press, 1997.

English translation of a German guide to the whiskeys of the world. Thousands of brands and terms listed and explained. Excellent quick-reference guide.

Jackson, Michael.

WHISKEY.

New York: Dorling Kindersley, 2005.

Heavily detailed and beautifully laid-out guide to the whiskeys of the world, including the new craft distillers. Required addition to any serious distiller's library.

Jackson, Michael.

THE WORLD GUIDE TO WHISKY.

Topsfield, MA: Salem House Publishers, 1988. The Bard of Brew's first take on the whiskeys of Scotland, Ireland, Canada, the United States, and Japan. A worthy companion to his seminal *The World Guide to Beer.*

MacLean, Charles.

WHISKEY (EYEWITNESS COMPANIONS).

London: Dorling Kindersley, 2008.

Lightweight but up-to-date listing of all major and a sprinkling of smaller whiskey distilleries worldwide, with limited tasting notes. Heavily illustrated in the patent DK publication style.

Murphy, Brian.

THE WORLD BOOK OF WHISKEY.

Chicago: Rand McNally & Co., 1979.

Interesting view of the whiskeys of the world just before the late twentieth-century rash of mergers, closures, and brand changes. *Après moi, le deluge.*

An old truck outside Stranahan's Colorado Whiskey.

Murray, Jim.

THE COMPLETE GUIDE TO WHISKEY.

Chicago: Triumph Books, 1997.

More properly a guide to Scotch, Irish, Canadian, and American whiskeys, and the distilleries that make them. Good capsule histories of the distilleries with minimal tasting notes.

Murray, Jim.

JIM MURRAY'S WHISKEY BIBLE.
London: Carlton Books. 2006 to date—Annual updates.

Close to all-encompassing pocket tasting guide to the world's whiskeys from Britain's other leading spirits writer.

WHISKEY, AMERICAN— GENERAL

Getz, Oscar.

WHISKEY: AN AMERICAN PICTORIAL HISTORY.

New York: David McKay, 1978.

Excellent pictorial history of liquor and distilling in American society.

Waymack, Mark H., and James F. Harris.

THE BOOK OF CLASSIC AMERICAN WHISKEYS.

Chicago: Open Court, 1995.

Concise history of American whiskey and current distilleries with detailed tasting notes.

WHISKEY, AMERICAN— BIOGRAPHY

Green, Ben A.

JACK DANIEL'S LEGACY.

Nashville: Rich Printing, 1967.

Quasi-official biography of the founder of America's leading whiskey distillery.

Krass, Peter. Blood & Whiskey:

THE LIFE AND TIMES OF JACK DANIEL.

Hoboken, NJ: John Wiley & Sons, 2004.

Interesting analysis of the life of Jack Daniel and his business world.

McDougall, John and Gavin D. Smith.

WORT, WORMS & WASH-BACKS: MEMOIRS FROM THE STILLHOUSE.

Glasgow: Angel's Share, 1999.

A sort of *Kitchen Confidential* of the Scotch distilling industry, with many droll and score-settling anecdotes from a veteran distiller and distillery manager.

Pacult, F. Paul.

AMERICAN STILL LIFE: THE JIM BEAM STORY.

Hoboken, NJ: John Wiley & Sons, 2003.

Standard recap of American whiskey distilling history with an emphasis on the growth of the Jim Bean Distillery and its brands.

Paterson, Richard, and Gavin D. Smith.

GOODNESS NOSE: THE PASSIONATE REVELATIONS OF A SCOTCH WHISKY MASTER BLENDER.

Glasgow: Angel's Share, 2010.

The autobiography of a master blender who has worked at a number of Scotch distilleries and has experienced the boom-and-bust cycles of the industry.

Taylor, Richard.

THE GREAT CROSSING: A HISTORIC JOURNEY TO BUFFALO TRACE DISTILLERY.

Frankfort, KY: Buffalo Trace Distillery, 2002.

Well-written company history with good insights into the development of bourbon distilling in early Kentucky.

Van Winkle Campbell, Sally.

BUT ALWAYS FINE BOURBON: PAPPY VAN WINKLE AND THE STORY OF OLD FITZGERALD.

Louisville: Limestone Lane Press, 1999.

Self-satisfied family history with lots of pretty pictures.

WHISKEY, AMERICAN— BOURBON & TENNESSEE

Carson, Gerald.

THE SOCIAL HISTORY OF BOURBON.

Lexington: University Press of Kentucky, 1984.

The evolving role of bourbon in America's collective lifestyle.

Cecil, Sam K.

THE EVOLUTION OF THE BOURBON WHISKEY INDUSTRY IN KENTUCKY.

Paducah, KY: Turner Publishing, 1999.

County-by-county listings and capsule histories of every distillery to operate in Kentucky. An obvious labor of love.

Cowdery, Charles K.

BOURBON, STRAIGHT: THE UNCUT AND UNFILTERED STORY OF AMERICAN WHISKEY.

Chicago: Made and Bottled in Kentucky, 2004.

An independent and frequently irreverent view of the American bourbon industry. Required reading for all serious students of American whiskey distilling.

Cowdery, Charles K.

BOURBON, STRANGE: SURPRISING STORIES OF AMERICAN WHISKEY.

Chicago: Made and Bottled in Kentucky, 2014.

A collection of droll, idiosyncratic, mostly historic essays on bourbon whiskey and the American whiskey industry.

Crowgey, Henry G.

KENTUCKY BOURBON: THE EARLY YEARS OF WHISKEYMAKING.

Lexington: University Press of Kentucky, 2008.

More properly a remarkably detailed history of the development of commercial distilling in Colonial America and the early United States. Substantial original scholarship. Who knew that peach brandy was once produced by most Southern whiskey distillers?

Barrels roll out at Woodford Reserve Distillery.

Barrels set for aging tequila in the warehouse/
tasting room at the Casa Cofradia Distillery, in
Tequila, Jalisco, Mexico.

Givens, Ron.

**BOURBON AT ITS BEST: THE LORE
AND ALLURE OF AMERICA'S FINEST
SPIRITS.**

Cincinnati: Clerisy Press, 2008.

Lavishly illustrated coffee-table book
introduction to bourbon.

Minnick, Fred.

**BOURBON CURIOUS: A SIMPLE
TASTING GUIDE FOR THE SAVVY
DRINKER.**

Minneapolis: Zenith Press, 2015.

And it is indeed simple.

Mitenbuler, Reid.

**BOURBON EMPIRE: THE PAST AND
FUTURE OF AMERICA'S WHISKEY.**

New York: Penguin Books, 2015.

A business-oriented history of the American
whiskey industry. Not quite an exposé, but
certainly a peek behind the curtains in the
stillhouses of a number of commercial
distilleries.

Murray, Jim.

**CLASSIC BOURBON, TENNESSEE AND
RYE WHISKEY.**

London: Prion Books, 1996.

An Englishman tastes American whiskeys
and likes them. Extensive tasting notes.

Murray, Jim.

JIM MURRAY'S WHISKY BIBLE.

Various: Various, 2004 to date.

An annual tasting and rating guide to the
whiskeys of the world. The taste descriptors
can sometimes be a bit exuberant, but this
is, far and away, the most extensive and
current guide to brands of whiskey in the
marketplace.

Regan, Gary, and Mardee Haidin Regan.

THE BOOK OF BOURBON.

Shelburne, VT: Chapters Publishing, 1995.

Extensive tasting notes, somewhat dated at
this point, with recipes.

Regan, Gary, and Mardee Haidin Regan.

THE BOURBON COMPANION.

Philadelphia: Running Press, 1998.

CliffsNotes for virtually all current brands
of bourbon.

WHISKY, CANADIAN

Bingham, Madeleine.

KING OF THE CASTLE: THE MAKING OF A DYNASTY: SEAGRAM'S AND THE BRONFMAN EMPIRE.

New York: Athenaeum, 1979.

The dirt on the now vanished dominant force in Canadian distilling.

Bronfman, Samuel.

FROM LITTLE ACORNS: THE STORY OF DISTILLERS

Corporation-Seagram, Ltd. Montreal: Distillers Corporation-Seagram Limited, 1970.

The Grand Old Man of Canadian distilling tells a cleaned-up version of the history of Seagram's and Canadian whiskey. Nary a mention of Joe Kennedy and bootlegging.

Brown, Lorraine.

200 YEARS OF TRADITION: THE STORY OF CANADIAN WHISKY.

Toronto: Fitzhenry & Whiteside, 1994.

A non-Seagram-centric history of Canadian whisky. A bit on the short side.

Marrus, Michael R.

SAMUEL BRONFMAN: THE LIFE AND TIMES OF SEAGRAM'S MR. SAM.

Boston: University Press of New England, 1991.

Academic analysis of the Canadian distilling industry through an overview of the now dismantled Seagram's whiskey empire.

Rannie, William F.

CANADIAN WHISKY: THE PRODUCT AND THE INDUSTRY.

Lincoln, ON: W. F. Rannie Publisher, 1976.

Interesting snapshot of the Canadian distilling industry on the eve of the late-twentieth-century industry consolidation.

WHISKEY, ASIA

Van Eycken, Stefan.

WHISKY RISING: THE DEFINITIVE GUIDE TO THE FINEST WHISKIES AND DISTILLERS OF JAPAN.

Kennebunkport, ME: Cider Mill Press, 2017.

The rapid evolution of grain spirits production in Japan from rather raw white spirits such as *shochu* to very smooth mature malt whiskeys is detailed in this instant standard reference work.

Sandhaus, Derek.

BAIJIU: THE ESSENTIAL GUIDE TO CHINESE SPIRITS.

Melbourne: Penguin Viking, 2014.

The world's best-selling spirit, by volume at least, is an acquired taste for most non-Chinese drinkers. This enthusiast's guide to the production, varieties, and major brands of baijiu is brisk and to the point.

WHISKEY, MOONSHINE— HISTORY

Carr, Jess.

THE SECOND OLDEST PROFESSION: AN INFORMAL HISTORY OF MOONSHINING IN AMERICA.

Englewood Cliffs, NJ: Prentice-Hall, 1972.

The history of moonshining, primarily in Southern states.

Dabney, Joseph Earl.

MORE MOUNTAIN SPIRITS.

Asheville, NC: Bright Mountain Books, 1980.

There is more to moonshine than just corn whiskey; peach brandy, for example. Chock-full of recipes and homemade still designs.

Dabney, Joseph Earl.

MOUNTAIN SPIRITS.

Asheville, NC: Bright Mountain Books, 1974.

A social history of Appalachian moonshine distilling with an attitude. Corn whiskey: good; sugar distillation: bad.

Keller, Esther.

MOONSHINE: ITS HISTORY AND FOLKLORE.

New York: Weathervane Books, 1971.

Moonshine in Kentucky and southern Indiana. Lightweight, but entertaining.

Mauer, David W.

KENTUCKY MOONSHINE.

Lexington: University Press of Kentucky, 1974.

Moonshining as an industry, from Colonial times to the present.

Owens, Bill.

MODERN MOONSHINE TECHNIQUES.

Hayward: White Mule Press, 2009.

The founder of the American Distilling Institute explains how to build a (very) simple distillery in your garage and make moonshine.

Spoelman, Colin, and David Haskell.

THE KINGS COUNTY GUIDE TO URBAN MOONSHINING: HOW TO MAKE AND DRINK WHISKEY.

New York: Abrams Books, 2013.

In this case, in New York City, rather than rural Tennessee. A pioneer craft distiller explains, in great detail, how a hobby became a lifestyle.

Rowley, Matthew.

LOST RECIPES OF PROHIBITION.

New York: The Countryman Press, 2015.

An actual Prohibition-era moonshiner's production manual reproduced, with annotations. Bathtub gin explained!

WHISKEY, IRISH

Magee, Malachy.

IRISH WHISKEY: A 1000 YEAR TRADITION.

Dublin: O'Brien Press, 1998.

Short but detailed history of Irish whiskey distilling, with capsule histories of every commercial distillery in Ireland.

McGuffin, John.

IN PRAISE OF POTEEN.

Belfast: Applegate Press, 1978.

Moonshine, Irish style. As is usually the case, romantic history is better than the rather squalid current state of affairs, with kitchen stills in urban housing estates distilling fermented sugar water.

McGuire, E. B.

IRISH WHISKEY.

Dublin: Gill & Macmillan, 1973.

A last-hurrah view of the Irish distilling industry, just prior to the final industry consolidation.

Murray, Jim.

CLASSIC IRISH WHISKEY.

London: Prion Books, 1998.

More or less complete tasting and buying guide to Irish whiskey, including local brands. Murray does tend to like everything, though.

Townsend, Brian.

THE LOST DISTILLERIES OF IRELAND.

Glasgow: Neil Wilson, 1999.

Companion book to the author's *Scotch Missed: The Lost Distilleries of Scotland*, only sadder. Scotland still has around a hundred distilleries, while Ireland, until recent industry revival, had been down to only three.

WHISKY, SCOTCH

Barnard, Alfred.

THE WHISKY DISTILLERIES OF THE UNITED KINGDOM.

Edinburgh: Birlinn, 2003.

Reprint of 1887 guide to the distilleries of Scotland, England, and Ireland. Wonderful window into a long-vanished world of distilling, with many engravings. A must-have for the historically minded distiller.

Brander, Michael.

THE ESSENTIAL GUIDE TO SCOTCH WHISKY.

Edinburgh: Canongate Publishing, 1990.

Compact report on the state of the Scottish distilling industry, circa 1990.

Cooper, Derek.

A TASTE OF SCOTCH.

London: Andre Deutsch, 1989.

The role of Scotch whisky in various facets of British culture. Lots of great graphics.

Daiches, David.

SCOTCH WHISKY: ITS PAST AND PRESENT.

New York: Macmillan, 1970.

The world of Scotch whisky distilling, just prior to the late-twentieth-century shutdowns.

Graham, Duncan, and Wendy Graham.

VISITING DISTILLERIES, 2ND EDITION.

Glasgow: Angel's Share, 2003.

Does your favorite Highland distillery have a gift shop? How clean is the loo? All your Whisky Trail questions are answered here.

Greenwood, Malcolm.

A NIP AROUND THE WORLD: THE DIARY OF A WHISKY SALESMAN.

Argyll: Argyll Publishing, 1995.

Stories from the front of whisky selling in Europe. Interesting but short.

Gunn, Neil M.

WHISKY & SCOTLAND: A PRACTICAL AND SPIRITUAL SURVEY.

Edinburgh: Souvenir Press, 1988.

Scotch Malt Whisky Society reprint of 1935 classic tome on Scotch whisky production and history.

Hume, John R., and Michael S. Moss.

THE MAKING OF SCOTCH WHISKY, REVISED EDITION.

Edinburgh: Canongate, 2000.

A business history of Scottish distilling. Very detailed, yet well written.

Jackson, Michael.

MICHAEL JACKSON'S COMPLETE GUIDE TO SINGLE MALT SCOTCH, 5TH EDITION.

Philadelphia: Running Press, 2004.

The benchmark guide to single malt Scotch whiskies, with more than a thousand tasting notes. A must-have reference book.

Jackson, Michael.

SCOTLAND AND ITS WHISKIES.

New York: Harcourt, 2001.

A travel guide to the various distilling regions of Scotland. Lovely photographs and lyrical text from Britain's leading spirits and beer writer.

Lockhart, Sir Robert Bruce.

SCOTCH: THE WHISKY OF SCOTLAND IN FACT AND STORY.

London: Putnam, 1970.

A standard history of Scotch whisky, much used (quoted and otherwise) by subsequent books on the topic.

MacLean, Charles.

MACLEAN'S MISCELLANY OF WHISKY.

London: Little Books, 2004.

A collection of whiskey-themed essays on a wide variety of topics. Great bedside book.

MacLean, Charles.

THE MITCHELL BEAZLEY POCKET WHISKY BOOK.

London: Mitchell Beazley, 1993.

Pocket guide with ratings on single malt, grain, and blended Scotch whiskies. Now somewhat dated.

McDougall, John, and Gavin D. Smith.

WORT, WORMS & WASH-BACKS: MEMOIRS FROM THE STILL-HOUSE.

Glasgow: Angel's Share, 2000.

Journeyman still master's tales of life in a variety of Scottish distilleries. Old slights and scores are settled in a most amusing manner.

McDowall, R. J. S.

THE WHISKIES OF SCOTLAND.

New York: Abelard-Schuman, 1967.

Distilleries, blenders, and their whiskeys of the time are described in extensive detail, while American mixers are denounced as foul pollutants of pure malt spirits.

Milroy, Wallace.

WALLACE MILROY'S MALT WHISKY ALMANAC.

New York: St. Martin's Press, 1991.

Limited tasting notes on single malt whiskeys from an early British advocate of the style.

Morrice, Philip.

THE SCHWEPPES GUIDE TO SCOTCH.

Sherborne, UK: Alphabooks, 1983.

All-encompassing guide to every Scotch distiller, blender, merchant, bottler, and marketing group. Somewhat outdated now, but still a useful reference guide.

Reeve-Jones, Alan.

A DRAM LIKE THIS . . .

London: Elm Tree Books, 1974.

Droll social history of Scotch with extensive mixed-drink and food recipes.

Townsend, Brian.

SCOTCH MISSED: SCOTLAND'S LOST DISTILLERIES, 3RD EDITION.

Glasgow: Angel's Share, 2004.

The life and death of more than a hundred Scottish distilleries are chronicled with photographs and directions. Try cross-referencing it with Barnard's The Whisky Distilleries of the United Kingdom.

THE DISTILLER'S GLOSSARY

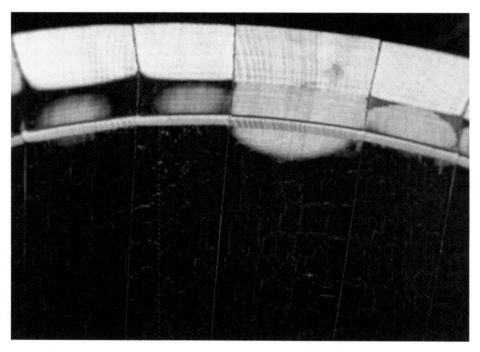

Detail of a charred barrel.

AGITATOR: A device such as a stirrer that provides complete mixing and uniform dispersion of all components in a mixture. Agitators are generally used continuously during the cooking process and intermittently during fermentation.

ALCOHOL: The family name of a group of organic chemical compounds composed of carbon, hydrogen, and oxygen; includes methanol, ethanol, isopropyl alcohol, and others.

APPLEJACK: In its original meaning, fermented hard apple cider that is partially frozen to separate the water from the alcohol. In modern terms, it is the North American version of apple brandy.

ATMOSPHERIC PRESSURE: Pressure of the air and atmosphere surrounding us that changes from day to day. It is equal to 14.7 psi.

AUGER: A rotating, screw-type device that moves material through a cylinder. In alcohol production, it is used to transfer grains from storage to the grinding site to the cooker.

BAKER'S YEAST: Standard robust yeast used openly by bakers and quietly by many distillers. The fermentation is quick and violent, and the resulting beer is cloudy. But that really doesn't matter if you are going to distill it.

BALLING: On a hydrometer, the measurement of the percent of sugar in a solution, by weight. See Brix.

BARREL: Varies depending on country. In U.S. terms, a unit of liquid measure equal to 42 American gallons or about 306 pounds; one barrel equals 5.6 cubic feet or 0.159 cubic meters. The standard bourbon cask usually holds between 53 and 55 gallons of spirit.

BATCH DISTILLATION: A process in which the liquid feed is placed in a single container and the entire volume is heated, in contrast to continuous distillation, in which the liquid is fed continuously through the still.

BATCH FERMENTATION: Fermentation conducted from start to finish in a single vessel.

BATCH PROCESS: Unit operation where one cycle of feed stock preparation, cooking, fermentation, and distillation is completed before the next cycle is started.

BATF: Formerly the Bureau of Alcohol, Tobacco, and Firearms; under the U.S. Department of Treasury. Responsible for the issuance of permits, both experimental and commercial, for the production of alcohol. The guns have been removed, and the agency has been renamed the Alcohol and Tobacco Tax and Trade Bureau (TTB).

BEER: A general term for all fermented malt beverages flavored with hops. A low-level (6 to 12 percent) alcohol solution derived from the fermentation of mash by microorganisms. For distillers, the initial fermented grain solution that is distilled. See Wash.

BEER STILL: The stripping section of a distillation column for concentrating ethanol.

BOILER: A unit base to heat water to produce steam for cooking and distillation processes.

BOURBON: Whiskey produced within the United States from a mash containing a minimum of 51 percent corn and then aged for a minimum of 2 years in a new charred oak barrel. Bourbon can be legally produced in any state.

BRANDY: Generally speaking, the result of distilling any fermented fruit wine. Specifically, the result of distilling grape wine. Fruit brandies are made from fruits other than grapes, while fruit-flavored brandies are usually grape brandy with added fruit flavors. See Eau de vie and Grappa.

BREWING: Generically, the entire beer-making process, but technically only the part of the process during which the beer wort is cooked in a brew kettle and during which time the hops are added. After brewing, the beer is fermented. In a grain distillery, the fermented wort or wash is frequently referred to as beer.

BRIX: A measurement of sweetness in a liquid, usually fruit juice. Specifically the measurement of dissolved sugar-to-liquid mass ratio of a liquid. As an example, in a 100-gram solution, a 30 Brix measurement is 30 grams of sugar and 70 grams of liquid.

BUBBLE-CAP TRAYS: Cross-flow trays usually installed in rectifying columns handling liquids free of suspended solids. The bubble caps consist of circular cups inverted over small vapor pipes. The vapor from the tray below passes through the vapor pipes into the caps and curves downward to escape below the rim into the liquid. The rim of each cap is slotted or serrated to break up the escaping vapor into small bubbles, thereby increasing the surface area of the vapor as it passes through the liquid.

CACHAÇA: Unaged, raw sugarcane spirit from Brazil, usually mixed with neutral grain spirit from other sources.

CANE SPIRIT: The broad term for spirits distilled from fermented sugarcane juice. See Cachaça and Rum.

COGNAC: By legal-definition, grape brandy from the Cognac region of France.

COLUMN: A vertical, cylindrical vessel used to increase the degree of separation of liquid mixtures by distillation or extraction.

COMPOUND: A chemical term denoting a combination of two or more distinct elements.

CONCENTRATION: The ratio of mass or volume of solute present in a solution to the amount of solvent. The quantity of ethyl alcohol (or sugar) present in a known quantity of water.

CONDENSER: A heat-transfer device that reduces a thermodynamic fluid from its vapor phase to its liquid phase.

CONTINUOUS FERMENTATION: A steady-state fermentation system that operates without interruption; each stage of fermentation occurs in a separate section of the fermenter, and flow rates are set to correspond with required residence times.

COOKER: A tank or vessel designed to cook a liquid or extract or digest solids in suspension; the cooker usually contains a source of heat and is fitted with an agitator.

COOKING: The process that breaks down the starch granules in the grain, making the starch available for the liquefaction and saccharification steps of the fermentation process.

COPRODUCTS: The resulting substances and materials that accompany the production of ethanol by distillation.

CORN WHISKEY (LIKKER): Legally: Minimum 80 percent corn mash whiskey, aged a minimum of 2 years in used wooden barrels. Illegally: the fresh-from-the-still original version of moonshine. See Moonshine.

CROSS-FLOW TRAYS: Liquid flows across the tray and over a weir to a downcomer that carries it to the next lower tray. Vapors rise from the bottom of the column to the top, passing through the tray openings and the pools of cross-flowing liquid.

DENATURE: The process of adding a substance to ethyl alcohol to make it unfit for human consumption; the denaturing agent may be gasoline or other substances specified by the Alcohol and Tobacco Tax and Trade Bureau.

DEWATERING: To remove the free water from a solid substance.

DISTILLATE: That portion of a liquid that is removed as a vapor and condensed during a distillation process.

Label for Cherry Liqueur by Clear Creek Distillery.

DISTILLATION: The process of separating the components of a mixture by differences in boiling point; vapor is formed by heating liquids in a vessel and successively condensing and collecting liquids with diferent boiling points.

EAU DE VIE: Colorless fruit brandy such as Kirschwasser from the Schwartzwald in Germany.

ETHANOL: The alcohol product of fermentation that is used in alcohol beverages and for industrial purposes; chemical formula blended with gasoline to make gasohol; also known as ethyl alcohol or grain alcohol.

ETHYL ALCOHOL: A flammable organic compound formed during sugar fermentation. It is also called ethanol, grain alcohol, or simply alcohol.

EVAPORATION: The conversion of a liquid to the vapor state by the addition of latent heat or vaporization.

FERMENTATION: A micro-organically mediated enzymatic transformation of organic substances, especially carbohydrates, generally accompanied by the evolution of a gas. The process in which yeast turns the sugars present in malted grains into alcohol and carbon dioxide.

GASOHOL (GASAHOL): Registered trade names for a blend of 90 percent unleaded gasoline with 10 percent fermentation ethanol.

GASOLINE: A volatile, flammable liquid obtained from petroleum that has a boiling range of approximately 29° to 216°C and is used for fuel for spark-ignition internal combustion engines.

GIN: White spirit flavored with juniper berry and other botanicals.

GRAPPA: A brandy distilled from grape pomace.

HEAD: The end (enclosure) of a cylindrical shell. The most commonly used types of heads are hemispherical, ellipsoidal, flanged and dished (semispherical), conical and flat.

HEADS: The initial run of distillate at the start of the distillation process. Heads are usually returned to the still for redistillation.

HEAT EXCHANGER: A unit that transfers heat from one liquid (or vapor) to another without mixing the fluids. A condenser is one type of heat exchanger.

HOPS: The dried blossom of the female hop plant (*Cumulus lupus*), which is a climbing herb. Aged hops are used by some whiskey distillers in the mashing process.

LAUTER TUN: The vessel used in brewing between the mash tun and the brew kettle. It separates the barley husks from the clear liquid wort. The barley husks themselves help provide a natural filter bed through which the wort is strained. This filtration is frequently skipped in grain distillation.

LAUTERING: The process of straining wort in a lauter tun before it is cooled in the brew kettle.

MASH: A mixture, consisting of crushed grains and water, that can be fermented to produce ethyl alcohol.

MASHING: The process by which barley malt is mixed with water and cooked to turn soluble starch into fermentable sugar. Other cereal grains, such as corn and rice, may also be added. After mashing in a mash tun, the mash is filtered through a lauter tun, whereupon it becomes known as wort.

METHYL ALCOHOL: A poisonous type of alcohol, also known as wood alcohol. Produced as a by-product of the fermentation of starch or cellulose. Methyl alcohol is not produced by fermenting sugar and only minimally from fruit wine.

MEZCAL: Distilled spirit from the pulp of the agave plant, produced in Mexico outside of the designated tequila production area. See Tequila.

MOONSHINE: Originally minimally aged corn whiskey produced illegally in the Appalachian Mountain region of the southern United States. Modern moonshine is usually made from fermented sugar water. See Corn whiskey.

POT: A hollow vessel more deep than broad.

PRESSURE VESSEL: A metal container, generally cylindrical or spheroid, capable of withstanding various loadings.

PROHIBITION: The process by which a government prohibits its citizens from buying or possessing alcoholic beverages. Specifically, Prohibition refers to the period between the effective date of the 18th Amendment to the U.S. Constitution (January 16, 1920) and its repeal by the 21st Amendment. Repeal took effect on December 5, 1933, although it was ratified by Congress in February, and the sale of beer was permitted after April 7, 1933.

PROOF: Alcohol containing 50 percent alcohol by volume (ABV) is called 100 U.S. proof spirit. U.S. proof is twice the percentage of spirit by volume.

RECTIFICATION: With regard to distillation, the selective increase of the concentration of the lower volatile components in a mixture by successive evaporation and condensation.

RECTIFYING COLUMN: The portion of a distillation column above the feed tray in which rising vapor is enriched by interaction with a countercurrent falling stream of condensed vapor.

RUM: A distilled spirit made from fermented molasses or sugarcane juice.

RYE WHISKEY: Whiskey containing a minimum of 51 percent rye grain, aged for at least 2 years in a new charred oak barrel. Rye whiskey, which was the original whiskey in Colonial America, has a dry, hard-edged palate, and is nowadays primarily blended into other types of whiskey to give them more character.

SHELL: Structural element made to enclose some space. Most shells are generated by the revolution of a plane curve.

SHOWER-TYPE TRAYS: These trays do not have downcomers. The liquid level results from the pressure drop caused by the counter-flowing streams.

Label for Bardenay Rum

SIEVE TRAYS: Sieve trays are usually cross-flow type perforated with small holes. Sieve trays are sometimes used for feeds that tend to deposit solids or polymerize in the column.

SIGHT GAUGE: A clear, calibrated cylinder through which liquid level can be observed and measured.

SLOBBER BOX: Pressure relief and particulate matter filter chamber located between the still and condenser coils on a pot still.

STILL: An apparatus for distilling liquids, particularly alcohols; it consists of a vessel in which the liquid is vaporized by heat, and a cooling device in which the vapor is condensed.

STRIPPING COLUMN: The section of the distillation column in which the alcohol concentration in the starting beer solution is decreased. This section is below the beer injection point.

STRIPPING SECTION: The section of a distillation column below the feed in which the condensate is progressively decreased in the fraction of a more volatile component by stripping.

TAILS: The final discharge of the distillation process, tails contain undesirable flavor elements (congeners) and fusel oils, and they are usually discarded.

TANK: A vessel of large size to contain liquids.

TEQUILA: Distilled spirit from the fermented pulp of the agave plant, produced by legal definition only in certain designated areas in and around the Mexican state of Jalisco. See Mezcal.

TUNNEL-CAP TRAYS: Tunnel-cap trays are similar to bubble-cap trays except that they are rectangular.

VALVE TRAYS: Valve trays are cross-flow trays with large perforations that are covered with flat plates. The cover plates are free to move vertically and thus permit the passage of ascending vapors.

VAPORIZATION: The process of converting a compound from a liquid or solid state to the gaseous state. Alcohol is vaporized during the distillation.

VESSEL: A container or structural envelope in which material is processed, treated or stored; for example, pressure vessels, reactor vessels, agitator vessels, and storage vessels (tanks).

VODKA: In U.S. terms, colorless, odorless, tasteless neutral spirit. Foreign vodkas can retain flavor elements, particularly if pot distilled.

WASH: In distilling, the liquid produced by the fermentation process, which is then distilled to concentrate the alcohol. See Beer.

WORM: Copper condenser coils suspended in a vessel of continuously flowing cold water, used as part of a pot still.

WORT: An oatmeal-like substance consisting of water and mash barley in which soluble starch has been turned into fermentable sugar during the mashing process. The liquid remaining from a brewing mash preparation following the filtration of fermentable beer. In grain distillation, the wort or mash is frequently fermented and then distilled without filtration.

YEAST: The enzyme-producing one-celled fungi of the genus *Saccharomyces* that is added to wort before the fermenting process for the purpose of turning fermentable sugar into alcohol and carbon dioxide.

INTERNATIONAL DIRECTORY OF DISTILLERIES

Way too many to list in print these days. For a reasonably current update please go to the American Distilling Institute website: www.distilling.com

ABOUT THE CONTRIBUTORS

ALTHOUGH it may seem that Alan Dikty wrote every word in this book and that Bill Owens took every photograph, that is not the case. The following collection of the usual suspects had a hand in it all, for which we are very grateful.

MIKE MCCAW

Mike McCaw is a cofounder and director of the Amphora Society and the coauthor of *The Compleat Distiller*, widely recognized as the primary technical publication concerning all aspects of small-scale distillation. McCaw now spends most of his time consulting with start-up craft and microdistillers and designing and building equipment for their operations. His current research is on further increasing the efficiency and lowering the carbon and water footprints of distilling processes. A book is in preparation detailing some of these techniques. He is working to create a series of hands-on workshops for aspiring distillers and also on stirring up grassroots interest in legalization of private, noncommercial distillation in the United States.

MATTHEW B. ROWLEY

Matthew Rowley is an advertising executive, former museum curator, and past board member of the Southern Foodway Alliance. He has traveled extensively in search of amateur and craft distillers to uncover local liquor and, when possible, promote those who make it.

He has spoken on distilling and cocktail culture for universities, radio, television, and the annual Tales of Cocktail in New Orleans. His essays and recipes have been published by the University of North Carolina Press, the University of Georgia Press, Simon & Schuster, the Taunton Press, Lark Books, and others. He has consulted on distilling-related broadcasts for the Fox network and the National Geographic Channel in the United States and RTE in Ireland.

Rowley lives in San Diego, California, where he maintains a 2000-volume culinary library open to chefs, bartenders, distillers, historians, journalists, and students. He is the author of *Moonshine!* (2007), a small batch distilling history/practicum for novices and publishes Rowley's Whiskey Forge (www.whiskey forge.com), a blog devoted to the history and practice of distilling, mixology, and good eats.

IAN SMILEY

Ian Smiley, BSc, is a research distiller and the author of *Making Pure Corn Whiskey*, an Amphora Society publication, and the owner of Smiley's Home Distilling at www. home-distilling. com, a web store dedicated to home and laboratory distillers. He has been exploring small-scale beverage-alcohol distillation all his adult life, and he is a card-carrying member of the American Distilling Institute (ADI). He's written articles for their magazine, *The American Distiller*, and was a major contributor to the recently published ADI book, *Craft Whiskey Distilling*. He is now part owner of a whiskey distillery in China, L.S. Moonshine, which is currently producing a corn whiskey white dog to satisfy the Chinese people's curiosity

for traditional American moonshine. L.S. Moonshine has other spirits planned for the Chinese market. In the future, Smiley plans to write books on making schnapps, brandy, and rum, and to continue his activities in commercial artisan distilling. He lives in Nepean, Ontario, Canada.

MAX WAXMAN

Max Waxman is the author of *Chasing the White Dog: An Amateur Outlaw's Adventures in the Moonshine Trade*, which will be published by Simon and Schuster in early 2010. His book *Race Day: A Spot on the Rail with Max Watman* (Ivan R. Dee) was called "a great tribute to American thoroughbred racing" and was an Editors' Choice in *The New York Times Book Review*.

He was the horse racing correspondent for the *New York Sun*, and wrote frequently on books, music, food, and drink for their Arts & Letters pages. He has written for the New York Times, *The New York Times Book Review*, Forbes FYI, *The Wall Street Journal*, *Fortune Small Business*, *Gourmet*, and *Parnassus*.

He was raised in the mountains of Virginia, and has worked as a cook, a farmer, a silversmith, a tutor, a greenskeeper, and a warehouseman. For a short time, he taught goat milking. He was educated at many schools and managed to graduate from Virginia Commonwealth University and Columbia University.

In 2008, Waxman was awarded a National Endowment for the Arts literary fellowship.

ACKNOW-LEDGMENTS

EARLIER VERSIONS of some of the text in this book previously appeared in various publications of the Beverage Testing Institute, and it is used here with the permission of BTI director Jerald O'Kennard and our grateful thanks.

Bill Owens cannot draw worth a damn, so we had Catherine Ryan redo his primitive sketches in a much more polished manner. They look great.

Amber Hasselbring serves as Bill's assistant and caregiver. Whatever he is paying her, it is not enough. The woman is a saint. Mixing a proper drink is truly an art, and Mark Gruber of Southern Wine & Spirits, Illinois, confirmed his artistic talent by reviewing and correcting our mixed drink recipes, as needed. The man even writes tasty.

ABOUT THE AUTHORS

ALAN S. DIKTY

Alan is the author of *The Buying Guide to Spirits* and numerous articles on distilling and brewing. In his spare time, he manages Allied Beverage Tanks, Inc., a company that builds craft breweries and distilleries. His current choice for a desert island dram is either Macallan 18-Year-Old Scotch Whisky or Rittenhouse 23-Year-Old Rye Whiskey, but he is open to alternatives.

ANDREW FAULKNER

Faulkner grew up in Carmel, California, reading the daybooks of Edward Weston, keeping journals, visiting Ansel Adams, and studying other black-and-white master photographers. His photo career diverted into journalism, getting a BA from California State University, Northridge, in 1993 and working for a dozen years in newspapers and magazines. Faulkner thought he had come full circle in 2005 when he started working for Bill Owens, one of the photographers whose art he followed as a teenager. His responsibilities at the American Distilling Institute grew as he became the managing editor of *Distiller* magazine in 2013 and publisher in 2018. He has come full circle into journalism. When Faulkner is not concerned with deadlines, punctuation, and correct spelling of names, he likes to play chess with his son, dance with his daughter, ride bikes with his wife, and make pretty pictures.

BILL OWENS

When he was not busy being an award-winning photographer or the founder of the brewpub industry in the United States, he somehow also found the time to be the author of an assortment of books and pamphlets on brewery and distillery operations, published by ADI. In his spare time, he tries his best to avoid personal responsibilities. www.distilling.com

INDEX

Ableforth's Bathtub Gin, 95
Absent Minded, 144
Absinthe, 144–145
Absinthe Verte, 144
Acetaldehyde, 42
Act of Union (1707), 68
Agave spirits, 132–138
Agave tequila, 137
Age-dated blended rums, 124
Agitator, 38
Aguardiente, 138
Air-conditioning, rum and, 122
Alambic Armagnacais, 108, 109, 114
Alambic charentais still, 36–37, 106
Alberta, Canada, 58, 62
Alcohol and Tobacco Tax and Trade Bureau (TTB), 16
Aldehydes, 42
Alembic stills, 30, 36, 37, 91. *See also* Alambic charentais still
Amari, 146–147
American Cask Strength Single-Malt Whiskey, 57
American Distilling Institute (ADI) founding of, 10
  Judging of Craft Spirits, 52, 87, 92, 96, 99, 101, 105, 107, 109, 114, 119, 122, 123, 125, 142, 143
Amodeo, Francesco, 146, 147
Anchor Brewing, 15
Andalusia Whiskey Co., 62
Añejo/Aged tequila, 71, 138
Anise-flavored spirits, 144
Antigua, 130
Anti-Saloon League, 50
Apple brandy, 71, 105, 113, 117, 118, 119
Applejack, 119
Aristotle, 13

Armaganc Castarede Reserve de la Famille, 108
Armenia, 115
Arrack, 91
The Art of Distillation (French), 13
Asia, 87, 91, 131. *See also* specific country names
Aspiring and accomplished artisans, 23
Atelier Vie, 145
Australia, 14, 15, 73, 74, 75, 76, 77–78, 87, 131
Austria, 78, 130
Azeotrope, 29, 33

Babylon, 12
Backins, 46
Baijiu vodka, 89–91
Balcones Distilling, 57
Balkans, 117
Barbados, 128, 130
Barley-based whiskey, 70, 74
Barrel aged/aging, 67, 99, 127, 136
Barreled Grape Immature Brandy, 110
Batch-still process, 35, 42–46
Bathtub gin, 95
Bay rum, 129
Beaver Pond Distillery, 118
Becherovka, 146
Beer, 18, 19, 49
Beer stripper, 44
Beer-stripping run, 44
Begin-cut, 46
Belarus, 86
Belgium, 94, 96, 100
Belle Rose Double Barrel Rum, 123
Belmont Farm Distillery, 19, 20
Bignell, Peter, 77
Bitters, 140, 146
Blackberry Liqueur, 143
Black Note Amaro, 144

Black Walnut Liqueur, 143
Blanco tequila, 138
Blanton's Distilling Company, 50
Blended American whiskey, 56, 60, 65
Blended rums, 124
Blended Scotch whiskey, 68–69, 70, 73
Blends, liqueurs as, 141
Bloody Butcher red corn, 52
Bloody Mary, 88
Blue agave tequila, 137
Boiling points, 27, 29, 42
Bonded whiskey, 66
Bonny Doon Vineyards, 114
Bottled in Canada whiskies, 61
"Bottle in Bond," 66
Bouilleurs de cru, 107
Bouilleurs de cru (traveling stills), 14
Bourbon craft distilleries, 52, 62
Bourbon distilleries, 55, 64, 119
Bourbon Rubenesque, 53
Bourbon whiskey, 34, 49–52, 50, 51, 54, 60, 66, 71
Bourbon wooden barrels, 75, 138
Boyd & Blair Potato Vodka, 85
Brandy, 104–119
  cocktails, 119
  contemporary brandies, 114
  fruit brandies, 105, 117–119
  grape brandies, 105, 113, 114
  groupings of, 105
  origins, 104
  pomace brandies, 105, 116
  regions, 106–115
  types of, 105
Brandy Alexander, 119
Brandy de Jerez, 111
Brandy distillation, 33, 36, 44, 71
Bridges, Jeff, 17

British settlers, 30, 58
BroVo Spirits, 146
Bubble-cap trays, 31, 34, 38, 39, 41
Buffalo Trace Distillery, 50, 51
Bulk Canadian whiskies, 61
Bulleit Rye, 51
Butts, 111

Cajun Spirits Distillery, 131
Caledonia Spirits Barr Hill Vodka, 87, 96
California brandies, 114, 117
Calvados, 117
Campbeltown, Scotland, 78
Canada, 15, 16, 62, 87, 116, 130. *See also* North America
Canadian whiskey, 58, 61, 71
Cane Land Distilling, 122
Cannon Beach Distillery, 139
Canton Cooperage, 59
Carc de Gewurztraminer, 116
Caribbean molasses, 50, 58
Caribbean, the, 87, 121, 122, 128, 129
Cask Strength Bloody Red Corn Bourbon, 52
Catalyzer, 38, 41
Central America, 129
Central Standard Craft Distillery, 55
Central Standard Spirits Wisconsin Rye Vodka, 87
Charboneau Distillery, 131
Charboneau, Doug, 131
Charboneau, Jean Luc, 130
Chardonnay Barrel Reserve Gin, 98
Chateau de Maniban, 107
Chateau de Triac Single Vineyard Fiins Bois, 107
Chemical flavor compounds. *See* Congeners
Cherry brandies, 117

China, 13, 89–91

Chivas Brothers Ltd., 68

Cinco de Noviembre MEzcal, 137

Citadelle Reserve Gin, 99

Civil War, 14

Classic Margarita, 139

Classic Martini, 103

Classifications
North American whiskey, 60–61
tequila, 138
vodka, 84

Clear Creek Distillery, 15, 116, 119, 143

Cocktails, 79, 88, 94, 103, 119, 125, 139

Code of Federal Regulations (CFR), 60

Cognac, 36, 106, 107, 109, 111

Colkegan Single Malt Whiskey, 57

Colorado Pure Distilling, 84

Columbus, Christopher, 121

Column stills
bourbon and, 50
brandy produced in, 106, 114, 115
continuous-run column still, 34–35
gin produced in, 97, 102
Irish whiskey, 76
Japanese whiskey, 76
rum produced in, 128
Scotch whiskey, 68
vodka and, 83, 84

Commercial distillation, 14, 49, 82. See also Craft distilleries

Condenser, 14, 25, 28, 31, 32, 33, 34, 36, 37

Condensor coil (moonshine still), 31

Congeners, 42, 44

Contemporary brandies, 114

Continuous-run column still, 24, 34–35

Continuous-run distillation process, 42–46, 47

Cooley Distillery, 70

Copper Fox Distillery, 62, 63, 64

Copper, stills made of, 41

Cordials, 141

Core Vodka, 87

"Corn likker" moonshine, 16

Corn whiskey, 49, 56, 57, 61, 71

Corsair Artisan, 96

Corsair Distillery, 54

Cotton & Reed, 129

Craft brewers, 19

Craft distilleries, 15
agave spirits, 138
bourbon, 52, 62
brandy, 114
corn whiskey, 57
gin, 99, 102
grappa, 116
legal moonshine and, 21
in New Zealand and Australia, 74
rum, 129
whiskey, 54, 62, 64, 65, 69

Craft pomace brandies, 116

Crèmes, 141

Croatia, 96

Cuba Libre (Rum and Coke), 125

Cuba, rum production in, 128

Czech Republic, 146

Daiquiri, 125

Dampfwerk Distillery Co., 110, 142

Dark Northern Reserve Straight Whiskey, 55

Dark rums, 124

Dasylirion, 138

Degens, Sebastian, 117

Demerara rums, 128

Dephlegmator, 28, 40

Depth Charge, 79

Destillerie Weidenauer, 78

Diablo's Shadow Bourbon Whiskey, 53

Diablo's Shadow Navy Strength Rum, 124

Distillation/distilling
basic steps in process of, 42–43
batch-still process, 42–46
chemistry of, 29
continuous-run process of, 47

definition, 26

distilling timeline, 71

earliest written record of, 12

early history of, 12–13

evolving technology of, 13–14

of gin, 97

government regulation, 14–15

as a hobby, 15, 19

process, 27

of rum, 127

single-run distillation, 45–46

taxation on, 14

tequila, 136

two-run distillation, 44–45

of vodka, 84

Distilled Spirits Plant (DSP), 87

Distilleries/distillers. See also Craft distilleries
bourbon, 55, 65, 119
networking among, 20
primary job of, 26
Scottish whiskey, 68
whiskey, 51, 52, 64, 78

Distiller's Gin #6, 102

Doc Herson's Natural Spirits, 144

Domaine Charbay, 116

Dominican Republic, 121, 128

Don Ciccio & Figli, 146, 147

Dornkaat, 100

Double Barreled Bourbon, 51

Double Gold Medal, 87

Drouin, Christian, 107

Dry gin, 71, 94, 98, 100, 102

Dry Spiced Rum, 129

Dunedin, New Zealand, 74

Eastern Europe, 81, 83, 86, 117, 145

Eau de vie, 25, 105, 117

Eaux de vie, 117, 146

Economic distillers, 23

El Keynote Agave Spirit, 139

Elk Rider Bourbon Whiskey, 53

Elk Rider Crisp Gin, 101

End-cut, 45, 46

England, 13, 14, 15, 68, 69, 94, 96, 98, 99

Epic of Gilgamesh, 12

Esters, 42

Estonia, 86

Ethanol, 29, 42, 44

Ethyl carbamate (urethane), 41

Etter Distillerie, 78

Europe, 15, 100, 130. See also individual country names

European Union, 75, 78

Excise Act of 1823, 68

Farallon Gin Works Gin Farallon, 92

Farber, Daniel, 114

Farmaceutica di Santa Maria Novella, 146

Fasano, Jonathan, 147

Feints, 44

Fermentation, 18, 34, 42, 43, 66, 91, 136

Fernet Branca, 146

Fernet Michaud, 146

Fiji, 131

Finland, 86

Flag Hill Winery and Distillery, 146

Flavors/flavoring
bathtub gin, 95
fruit brandy, 105
gins/genever, 94, 96, 97, 99, 100, 102
liqueurs, 141
tequila, 136
vodkas, 88

Forsyths whiskey still, 33

France, 13, 14, 50, 86, 105, 106–109, 117, 130, 144

Fremont Mischief Distillery, 55

French Charentais alembic still, 30, 36–37

French, Jonathan, 13

Frozen Fruit Margarita, 139

Fruit brandies, 105, 117–119

Fruit bricks, 18

Fruit mashes, 38

Gabriel, Alexendre, 107

Gaelic culture, 67

Generic liqueurs, 143

Genever-styled gins, 71, 94, 96, 97, 98

George Dickel Rye, 51

Georgia (country), 115

Georgia (state), 50
Germain-Robin (craft distillery), 15, 105, 114
Germain-Robin, Hubert, 115
German immigrants, 49, 55
Germany, 13, 78, 86, 100, 112, 117, 119, 143
Gerrymandering, 15
Gin, 92–103
    barrel-aged, 99
    basis of, 94, 96
    bathtub gin, 95
    cocktails, 103
    distillation of, 97
    distilling timeline, 71
    history of, 93–96
    regions, 100–102
    styles, 98
Gin and Tonic, 103
Gin Craze, 14
Gin Lane (Hogarth), 93
Glenora, Nova Scotia, 62
Golden rums, 124, 130, 131
Gold tequila, 138
Gooseneck still, 32–33, 46
Grain mashes, 38, 91
Grain whiskey, 69, 73, 75, 76
Grand Marnier, 143
Grape brandy, 104, 105, 113, 114
Grape pomace, 37, 114
Grappa, 37, 71, 116
"Great Balls of Fire" (Wolfe), 17
Great Britain, 14, 122. See also England; Scotland
Great Lakes Distillery, 102
Great Southern Distilling Company, 74
Greece, 115, 144
Greece, ancient, 13
Green Brier Tennessee White Whiskey, 54
Green Fairy, 144
Green Hat Gin, 93
Guyana, 123, 128

Haik, Ed, 131
Haiti, 121, 128
Harvest Spirits Core Vodka, 87
Heads, 27, 28, 34, 35, 42, 44, 45, 47
Hearts, 34, 35, 42, 44, 45, 46,

47
Helgolander German style Herbal Liqueur, 142
Helmet, 36, 38, 39
Heritage Distilling Co., 53, 85, 101
Heron, Joe, 114
Heron, Lesley, 117
Herson, Kevin, 145
Heublein Company, 83
High Council Brandy, 113
HIghland malt whiskeys, 78
History of distilling, 12–21
    bourbon whiskey, 49–52
    brandy, 104
    craft distilleries, 15
    earliest known use of distillation, 12
    gin, 93–94
    Irish whiskey, 70
    Japanese whiskey, 72
    moonshine, 16–21
    New Zealand and Australian whiskies, 74
    North American whiskey, 59
    regulation of distilling, 14–15
    rum, 121–123
    Scotch whiskey, 67–69
    spread of knowledge and technology on, 13–14
    vodka, 81–84, 90, 91
    whiskey, 67–70
Hobbyist distillers, 15, 19. See also Home distilling
Hogarth, William, 93
Hokkaido, Japan, 77
Holland, 86, 91, 92, 94, 96, 100
Homebrewers, 19–20
Home distilling, 14–15, 16, 20, 21, 23, 31, 82
Honshu, Japan, 77
Hopi blue corn, 52, 57
Howell, Gillian, 70
Hudson Bay Bourbon, 50
Hungary, 146
Hybrid pot still, 30, 38–41, 45, 85, 102

Immigrants in North America, 49, 55

India, 15, 75, 91
Indiana, 50, 52, 55, 62, 65
India, whiskey in, 75, 76
Indonesia, 91
Infused spirits, 140–147
Inlander rum, 130
Internal steam coil, 25
International Judging of Craft Spirits, 87
Ireland, 13, 15, 49, 70, 104. See also Irish whiskeys
Irish Distillers Company (IDC), 70
Irish immigrants, 49, 55
Irish malt whiskey, 73
Irish pot still whisky, 73
Irish whiskeys, 32, 70–71, 73, 75, 76, 77
Island Orchard Eau de Vie Apple Brandy, 105, 118
Islay whiskeys, 77
Israel, 115
Italy, 13, 86, 96, 111, 116, 144, 146

Jack Daniel's Distillery, 54
Jackson Hole Still Works Highwater Vodka, 87
Jägermeister, 146
Jamaica, 128
Japan, 13, 48, 72, 73, 75, 76, 77, 87, 91
Japanese malt whiskey, 73
Jaxon Keys Winery, 114
Jenever, 94
Jepson Old Stock Brandy, 114
Jepson Vineyards, 15, 114
Johnny Ziegler Black Forest Style Apple Aux Pommel Schnapps Eau de Vie, 143
Johnson, Robert Glen Jr. (Junior Johnson), 17
Jos. A. Magnus & Co. Distillery, 56
Juniper-flavored gin, 92, 93, 94, 96, 97

Kahlúa, 143
Karuizawa Number One Single Cask Whisky, 72

Kentucky, 49, 50, 51, 52, 55, 62
Kettle, 32, 33, 36, 37, 38
Kill Devil, 121
Kimo Sabe Mezcal, 137
Kittling Ridge, Ontario, 62
Kiwi home distillers, 20
Kneiper, Rich, 118
Korbel, 114
Korea, soju in, 91
Korn, Germany, 78
Kubanskaya, 88
Kweichow Moutai, 89
Kymar Farm Winery and Distillery, 118

Labrot & Graham Distillery, 50
Laird & Co., 113
Laird's Distillery, 119
Lampglass, 28
Lancut Distillery, 143
Lao khao, 91
Latin America, 15, 115
Latvia, 86
Lawrenceburg, Indiana, 51
Legislation, 20, 93. See also Regulation
Leopold Bros., 115, 144, 147
Leopold Brothers Distillery, 146
Leopold, Todd, 147
Libya, ancient, 13
Limeburners Single Malt Whisky, 74
Limonnaya, 88
Liqueurs, 140, 141–143
Liquid Riot, 146
Lithuania, 86
London Dry Gin, 98, 102
Louisiana Spirits, 130
Lowe, Michael, 93
Lowland malt whiskeys, 77
"Low wine" spirits, 42, 43, 44, 45
Lyne arm, 25, 28, 32

Macallan Distillery, 68
Madagascar, 131
Mad River Distillers, 119
Maggie's Farm Rum Distillery, 130
Maison Ferrand, 107

Makers Mark Bourbon, 49
Malahat Spirits Cabernet Barrel Rum, 122
Malahat Spirits tasting room, 130
Malted barley, 18, 68, 74, 75
Malting, 91
Malt whiskey, 68, 69, 72, 73, 74, 75, 76, 77, 78
Malvados Apple Brandy, 119
Manhattan, 79
Manitoba, Canada, 62
Manuele Distillers KoHana Koho Hawaiian Agricole Rum, 122
Mao tai vodka, 89–90
Maple Liqueur, 142
Margarita, 139
Martini, 103
Martinique, 123, 127, 128
Maryland, 49, 55
Mash bills, 52, 58, 59
Mashing, 91
Mash/mashing, 18, 33, 34, 37, 38, 42, 43, 50, 66, 81
Mash tun, 43
Mauritius, 131
Maysville, Kentucky, 51
Maytag, Fritz, 15
McCool, Clark, 115
McMenamins Cornelius Pss Roadhouse (CPR) Distillery, 104
McMenamins CPR Distillery, 113, 115
Melazas, 121
Methanol, 42
Mexico, 115, 133, 134, 136, 138
Mezcals, 133, 134, 136, 137, 139
MGP of Indiana, 51
Middle West Spirits, 53
Miller, Chuck, 20
Missouri, 50
Mixtos, 136, 138
Modern "moonshiners," 19–20
Moersch, Rick, 113
Molasses, 50, 58, 81, 121, 122, 127
Montanya Distillers, 130
Moonshine, 16–25, 61
    corn whiskey, 57
    defined, 21

distilling timeline, 71
Junior Johnson and, 17
making, 18
modern production of, 16, 19–20, 23
New Zealand, 74
during Prohibition, 16, 18, 52
still, 31
Moor's cap, 40
Morris, Chris, 52
Mosby Vineyards, 116
Moscow Mule, 83
Mount Gay Distillery, 128
Moylan, Brendan, 137
Moylan's Brewing Co., 57
Mrs. Beeton's Book of Household Management, 94
Murray Hill Club Special Release Blended Bourbon, 56

NASCAR racing, 17
Nelson's Green Brier Distillery, 54
Neutral grain spirit (NGS), 83, 84
New Columbia Distillers, 93
New Deal Distillery, 105
New Jersey, 113, 119
New Zealand, 15, 20, 75, 76, 78
New Zealand blended whiskey, 73
New Zealand Single malt whiskey, 73
Nikka Whiskey Distillery, 72
North America, 15, 87, 102, 122, 129–130. See also Canada; United States
North American whiskey
    blended American whiskey, 56
    bourbon, 49–52
    Canadian whiskey, 58, 62
    classifications of, 60–61
    corn whiskey, 57
    craft distilleries, 65
    overview, 48, 59
    regions, 62
    Rye whiskey, 55
    Tennessee whiskey, 54
North Carolina, 17, 50

North Shore Distillery, 102
Notch Nantucket Island Single Malt Whiskey, 57
Nova Scotia, Canada, 62

Oceana rum, 131
Ogden's Own, 146
Ogee, 28
Ohio, 50
Okhotnichya, 88
Olathe corn, 52
Olbracht, King Jan, 82
Old Gristmill Authentic American Corn Whiskey, 78
Old Pogue Distillery, 51
Old Tom Gin, 98, 99
Old Tom style of gin, 94
Online forums, 20
Ontario, Canada, 58, 62
Orcas Island Distillery, 105, 118
Oregon, 99, 117, 138
Oregon Spirit Distillers, 144
Orr, Prentis, 85
Osocalis Distillery, 114
Ouzo, 144
OYO Sherry-Finished Bourbon Whiskey, 53

Pakistan, 13, 75, 76
Pappy Van Winkle's bourbon, 50, 51
Park Cognac, 107
Pastis, 144, 145
Pear brandies, 117
Pear Brandy, 105
Peated barley malt, 75
Peat fires, 68
Peat-smoked character, 72, 73, 74, 75
Penderyn Whisky Distillery, 70
Penedès brandy, 111
Pennsylvania, 49, 50, 55
Pennsylvania Pure Distillery, 85
Pernod, 144
Pertsovka, 88
Philippines, the, 131
Phylloxera infestation, 69, 113
Piedmont Distillers, 17
Pilgrims, 50

Pisco Punch, 115
Pisco Style Brandy, 115
Planter's Punch, 125
Plum brandy, 117
Plymouth Gin, 98
Pogue Distillery, 51
Pogue, John, 51
Poland, 13, 82, 84, 86
Pomace brandies, 105, 116
Poteen, 70
Pot stills, 20
    anatomy of, 24
    bourbon and, 50
    brandy produced in, 114, 115
    gin produced in, 102
    Irish whiskey, 76
    Japanese whiskey, 76
    New Zeland and Australia whiskey, 76
    rum production in, 128
    Scotch whiskey, 76
    used by artisans, 23
    vodka and, 83, 84
Preheater, 36–37
Prezydent Vodka, 82
Prichard's Distillery, 51, 130
Private distillation, 14–15. See also Home distilling
Prohibition, 15
    bourbon industry and, 50, 52
    fruit bricks and, 18
    gin and, 95
    grape brandy and, 113
    Irish whiskey and, 70
    moonshine and, 16
    rum and, 122
    rye whiskey and, 55
    vodka and, 83
Proprietaries (liqueurs), 143
Puerto Rico, 128
Purifier (dephlegmator), 28

Qu, 91
Quakers, 94
Quebec, Canada, 62

Ransom Old Tom Gin, 99
Raspberry brandies, 117
Raspberry Liqueur, 142
Recipes. See Cocktails

Reflux (condensation), 31, 32, 33, 40–41
Regions
  brandy, 106–115
  gin, 100–102
  rum, 128–131
  vodka, 86–87
  whiskey, 77–78
Regulation, 14–15, 59, 99, 141
Rehorst Premium Milwaukee Gin, 102
Reposado/Rested tequila, 138
Revere, Paul, 94
Reynolds, Burt, 17
Rhum Agricole LA Rum, 122
Richards, Andrew, 118
Richland Distilling Co., 126
RMS, 114
Rocky Mountain Peach Flavored Whiskey, 147
Rosolis Ziolowy Gorzki, 143
Rum, 120–131
  basis of, 120, 127
  cocktails, 125
  distillation of, 33, 127
  distilling timeline, 71
  history of, 121–123
  regions, 128–131
  styles of, 124
Rum and Coke, 125
Rummanger, 33
Rum verschnitt, 130
Ruqu de, 91
Russel, Jimmy, 52
Russia, 13, 81–82, 84, 86, 88
Rusty Nail, 79
Ryan, Bob, 124
Ryan & Wood Distillers, 124
Rye whiskey, 48, 49, 55, 60, 71

Sagaponack Farm, 87
Salish Sea Organic Liqueurs, 142
Sante Fe Spirits, 57
Sazerac, 79
Schnapps, 33, 38, 55, 143
Scotch grain whiskey, 73, 76
Scotch malt whiskey, 69, 76
Scotch whiskey, 67–69, 71
Scotland, 13, 15, 48, 49, 69, 77
Scottish immigrants, 49, 55

Scottish malt whisky, gooseneck still for, 32, 33
Scottish whiskey, 75, 76
Screech, 130
Screwdriver, 88
Seagram's Extra Dry gin, 102
Seagram's plant, 51
Sex On The Beach, 88
Shady Knoll Orchards and Distilling, 118118
Sidecar, 119
Sidetrack Distillery, 146
Sidetrack Distillery Raspberry Brandy, 117, 141
Siegried Herzog Destillate, 112
Silver tequila, 138
Sinedrius, 13
Single barrel bourbon, 60
Single Barrel Tennessee Single Malt Whiskey, 54
Single Malt Scotch Whisky, 69, 73
Skip Rock Distillers, 123, 142
Slivovitz Plum Brandy, 118
Sloe Gin, 95
SLYRS distillery, 112
Small batch bourbon, 60, 123
Smirnoff brand, 83
Solera system, 111, 114, 115
Sotol, 138
Sour mash, 50, 66
South Africa, 15, 115
South America, 115, 122, 129
Southern Comfort, 143
South Hollow Spirits, 125
Spain, 13, 88, 96, 100, 111
Spent wash, 29
Spiced rums, 124
Spigot, 14
Spirit run, 44–45, 46
Spirit still, 44
Stark Spirits, 118, 123
State 38 Distilling, 139
Steam jacket, 14, 33, 38
St. George Spirits, 15, 116, 144
Still(s)
  anatomy of a craft whiskey, 33
  blueprint of, 14, 28
  continuous-run column, 34–35
  design of whiskey, 30
  dimensions of a typical, 24

French Charentais alambic, 36–37
  gooseneck, 32–33
  moonshine, 31
  parts of a whiskey, 28
  for producing Cognac, 106
Stinger, 119
Stone Barn Brandyworks, 117
Straight Bourbon Whiskey, 53
Straight whiskey, 66
Stryker Smoked Single Malt Whiskey, 62
Sugarcane, 75, 120, 121, 122, 127, 131
Sugarcane juice, 127, 128, 131
Sugar House Distillery, 53
Sugar-maple charcoal, 54
Sunshine Orange Brandy, 118
Suntory Company, 72
Sutherland Distilling Co., 53, 124
Swan neck, on pot still, 25, 28
Sweden, 13, 76, 82, 86

Tahiti, 131
Tails, 28, 34, 35, 42, 44, 45, 46, 47
Taiwan whiskeys, 75, 76
Taketsura, Masataka, 72
Talisker whiskey, 69
Taxation, 14, 49, 57, 66, 70, 74
Taxila, 13
Technical distillers, 23
Temperance movement, 50
Temperature, boiling point, 27, 29, 42
Templeton Rye, 51
Tench, Keith, 70
Tennessee, 49, 50, 52, 62
Tennessee whiskey, 53, 54, 60, 71
Tequila, 132–139
  basis of, 134
  cocktails, 139
  distillation and aging of, 136
  distilling timeline, 71
  evolution of, 133–134
  fermentation stage, 136
  upgrading and upscaling of, 139
Tequila Sunrise, 139

Terra-cotta distillation system, 13
Thailand, 91, 131
Thujone, 145
Tito's Handmade Vodka, 84
Tom Collins, 103
Tom's Foolery Rye Whiskey, 55
Tormore Distillery, 68
Townshend's Distillery, 141
Traveling stills, 14
Trinidad, 128
Triple Eight Distillery, 57
True Blue Corn Whiskey, 57
Tullamore Drew, 70
Turin Vermouth, 144
Tuthilltown Spirits, 50
Twenty Boat Amber Rum, 125
Two James Distillery Barrel Reserve Old Cockney Gin, 98
Two-run distillation, 44–45

Ukraine, 86
Underground Herbal Spirit, 146
Unicum, 146
United Kingdom, 15, 86, 100, 130. See also England; Great Britain; Ireland; Scotland
United States. See also North America; North American whiskey
  apple brandy in, 119
  brandy produced in, 113–114
  craft distilleries, 15
  gin production in, 95
  moonshine production, 16
  pomace brandies, 116
  rum production in, 122, 129–130
  vodka in, 83–84, 87
Uralt, 112
Urethane, 41

Van Winkle III, Julian, 51
Vatted Malt Scotch Whiskey, 73
Vietnam, 90, 91
VINN Baiju, 90
VINN Distillery, 90, 91

Virginia, 49, 50, 52, 58, 62, 64, 113, 119
Virginia Lightning Corn Whiskey, 19
Virginia Sweetwater Moonshine, 21
Virgin Islands, 129
Virginia Lightning Moonshine, 19
Virginia Sweetwater Distillery, 21
Vodka, 80–91
  baijiu, 89–91
  basis of, 81
  classifications of, 84
  cocktails, 88
  distillation of, 84
  distilling timeline, 71
  flavored, 88
  flavors, 88
  history, 81–84
  produced in Asia, 89–91
  regions, 86–87
  technical distillers and, 23
Vonk, Erik and Karin, 126
VS (very superior) industry standard, 107
VSOP (very superior old pale) industry standard, 107
VSP (very superior pale) industry standard, 107

War of 1812, 14
Wash, 25, 28, 31, 33, 38, 43, 47
Washington, George, 14, 15, 49, 94
Washington Rye, 55
Wasmund, Rick, 64
Wasmund's Single Malt Whiskey, 65
Weidenauer, Oswald "Ossie," 78
Weinbrand, 112
Whiskey, 48–79. See also Moonshine
  Australian, 74
  basis of, 75
  blended American whiskey, 56, 60
  bonded, 66
  bourbon, 49–53, 60

Canadian whiskey, 58, 61
cocktails, 79
corn whiskey, 57, 61
craft distilleries, 54, 62, 64, 65, 69
  definition, 67
  history of North American, 59
  Irish, 32, 70–71, 73, 75, 76, 77
  Japanese, 72–73, 75
  labeling/labels, 50, 51
  mash, 66
  New Zealand, 74
  North American regions, 62–65
  overview, 48
  Pappy Van Winkle, 51
  regional flavors, 65
  regions, 77–78
  rye whiskey, 48, 49, 55, 60, 71
  Scotch whisky, 67–69, 71, 73, 76
  spelling, 49
  straight whiskey, 66
  Tennessee whiskey, 54
Whiskey distillation
  batch-still process, 44
  distilleries, 51, 52, 64
  by region, 76
  Tennessee whiskey, 54
  timeline, 71
Whiskey Rebellion of 1791, 14
Whiskey Sour, 79
Whiskey still, 25, 28, 30, 32, 33
"White dog," 21
White Lightning (film), 17
White rums, 122, 124
"White whiskey," 21
Wigle Whiskey, 144
Wildcard Absinthe, 144
Willett Distillery, 62
Winegarden Estate, 143
Winters, Lance, 71
Wise King Anejo Agave Spirit, 139
Witblits, 115
Wodo, Dave, 124
Wolfe, Tom, 17
Women's Christian Temperance Union, 50
Woodford Reserve Distillery, 9, 32, 50, 52, 63
Wood Hat Spirits, 52, 53, 143

Woodinville Whiskey Co., 53
Worm (condenser), 13, 25, 28
Worm (mezcal), 136
Wormwood, 145

XO (extra old) industry standard, 107

Young, Barry, 85

Zubrowka, 88